BORTHWICK INSTITUTE
UNIVERSITY OF YORK

Landscape and Society in the Vale of York, c.1500-1800

by

Brodie Waddell

BORTHWICK PAPER NO. 120

First Published 2011

© Brodie Waddell

ISSN: 0524-0913
ISBN: 978-1-904497-55-4

Acknowledgements

This paper is the product of an extremely pleasant year of research and writing in which I incurred many debts. My time at York was made possible by an extraordinarily generous bequest from Rena Fenteman, which funded the post-doctoral fellowship as well as the costs of research and publication. I am very grateful to Rena Fenteman and her trustees, Godfrey and Patricia Fenteman, for this opportunity and I hope my work will meet their expectations. My research would also have been impossible without the facilities and support provided the Borthwick Institute for Archives at the University of York. I thank Chris Webb, the Keeper of the Archives, and everyone else at the Borthwick for their help and for their patience despite my unfamiliarity with archival work. The staff at Department of History at the University of York, especially Professor Bill Sheils, deserve my gratitude too. I am also grateful to the people at the Victoria County History project, who welcomed me into the convivial world of local history research. Finally, I would like to extend thanks to all of the archivists and librarians who helped me along the way, including those at the University of York Library, the Doncaster Archives, the Hull History Centre, the John Goodchild Collection, the East Riding of Yorkshire Archives, the North Yorkshire County Record Office, The National Archives at Kew, the West Yorkshire Archive Service, the York City Archives, the York Minster Archives, and the Yorkshire Archaeological Society Archive. Of course, my greatest personal debt is owed to my wife, Danielle, for reasons too numerous to list.

The principal purpose of Rena Fenteman's bequest was to research the history of Barlow (near Selby), the village of her ancestors. This resulted in a history of the township, published online at http://www.victoriacountyhistory. ac.uk/Counties/Yorkshire-West-Riding by the Victoria County History project as a first contribution to a VCH of the West Riding of Yorkshire. However, Miss Fenteman recognised that Barlow's history is significant not primarily in itself, but for its place in the region of which it formed a part. Thus, this paper is intended illuminate the Vale of York as a whole, though with special attention paid to Barlow and its neighbours. I hope the paper will complement the township study by providing the context necessary for a fuller understanding of this locality.

Abbreviations

a.	acre
AHEW	*Agrarian History of England and Wales*
BIA	Borthwick Institute for Archives
d.	pence
DA	Doncaster Archives
HHC	Hull History Centre
NYCRO	North Yorkshire County Record Office
r.	rood
s.	shilling
TNA	The National Archives
VCH	*Victoria County History*
WYAS-B	West Yorkshire Archive Service, Bradford
WYAS-W	West Yorkshire Archive Service, Wakefield
YMA	York Minster Archives

Landscape and Society in the Vale of York, c. 1500-1800

Introduction

The Vale of York was a wealthy, densely populated, low-lying agricultural region throughout the early modern period. To a well-informed observer in 1546, it was 'one of the greatest and richest valleys that ever he found in all his travel though Europe'.[1] It was tightly integrated into national and international markets thanks to the navigability of the River Ouse and its tributaries, whilst also being well-served by the city of York, the capital of early modern northern England, and by several substantial market towns.[2] Yet, unlike many other regions in the county, the agrarian history of this part of Yorkshire has been mostly neglected by historians.

This study is therefore an attempt to sketch out some of the most notable features of early modern rural life in the region, especially the complex relationship between its people and its landscape. It begins, in part one, with an overview of the region as a whole, noting its key characteristics and comparing it to the rest of the county. The social and economic foundations of life in the Vale receive particular attention, but the role of religion and literacy in its culture are also assessed. This section provides context for the analysis that follows and will also, I hope, serve as a useful introduction to the Vale for those interested in local history, though a short paper is obviously bound to be far from comprehensive in its coverage. In part two, the focus shifts to the landscape itself. It consists of a survey of the built environment – housing, enclosures, roadways, waterways, drains and fences – and of the surrounding countryside – fields, meadows, woodlands and pastures. This analysis reveals the many ways in which land was shared and managed by the community, and how these uses and practices changed over the course of three centuries.

Figure 1 The Vale of York and Yorkshire

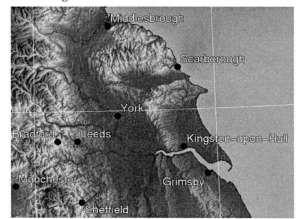

Source: Captain Blood, 'Topographic map of the United Kingdom', *Wikimedia Commons*, 7 July 2006 [http://commons.wikimedia.org/wiki/File:Uk_topo_en.jpg, accessed 12 November 2011].

The regional focus of this study should be apparent from its title, but some clarification may be helpful. Geographically, the 'Vale of York' referred to in the following pages might more correctly be called the 'Greater Vale of York' (Figure 1). It stretches down from the narrow floodplains around Northallerton, just a few miles south of the Tees, to the flat fenlands between Doncaster and the Trent, a total length of around eighty miles. It is bounded on the west by a long Magnesian Limestone ridge and on the east by the rising elevations of the North York Moors, the Howardian Hills and the Yorkshire Wolds. At its widest point, between Tadcaster and Market Weighton, it is only around twenty miles across, but it still encompasses a very substantial part of Yorkshire, covering a larger area than most entire counties. Within this region, there are essentially three sub-regions, each with their own chief towns and geographical peculiarities. The Vale of Mowbray, with a gently 'undulating' landscape, spreads out from Northallerton and Thirsk.[3] The central Vale is generally flatter (though crossed by two glacial moraines) and forms the hinterland of York itself as well as Selby.[4] The Humberhead Levels area is flatter still, with much of it below sea level, surrounding Howden and of course Doncaster.[5] Of these three sub-regions, the primary focus of this study is the mid-Vale, especially the fifty-two settlements situated along the

Figure 2 The Southern Vale of York and the Humberhead Levels

Source: OS OpenData.

River Ouse from its origin in the Ure at Linton-on-Ouse in the north to where it joins the Humber at Trent Falls in the south (Figure 2). Yet, it also includes numerous examples from other parts of the Vale and I believe that most of my conclusions apply to the whole of the region.

The sources upon which this paper is based are wide in scope. I devoted the greatest share of my research to records of this region's manorial courts, examining over 130 sets of regulations from 26 different manors. These are quantified in Appendix 1 and three transcriptions are included as examples in Appendix 2. In addition, I consulted estate papers from several landholders, probate inventories, parish registers, records of national and county courts, taxation figures, enclosure awards and plans, early census data, and the first Ordnance Surveys. Throughout this study, I have also used the work of previous historians in the form of scholarly books and articles, amateur local histories, and edited primary sources. The limited amount of time that I have spent with this material means that all of my assertions must be considered tentative, but I believe that these sources collectively offer a solid basis for investigating this topic. Through an examination and analysis of these records, we can learn much about the uniqueness of this region, the efforts of its inhabitants to control their environment, and the continual changes experienced by the Vale during a transformative period in English history.

Part 1. The Vale of York

The people of this district had a way of life quite distinct from the traditional stereotype of the Yorkshire experience. Despite their geographical proximity, the villages of the Vale of York shared very few of the social and economic features typical to the cloth towns of the Pennine foothills or the scattered upland settlements of the Yorkshire Dales and North York Moors.[6] Instead, the men and women who lived in the lowlands had much more in common with the people of other 'cattle and corn' areas spread throughout the Midland Plain.[7] Their numbers, wealth, social structure, livelihoods, and even cultural activities set them apart from much of northern England, giving them a unique place in the history of the county and of the nation as a whole.

1.1 Population and Wealth

Determining the population and prosperity of the Vale is very difficult prior to the nineteenth century, but a rough picture can be discerned by piecing together snap-shots provided by taxation records. The first glimpse of early modern Yorkshire came in 1524-25 though the lay subsidy returns.[8] These assessments make it clear that the people of the Vale were both more numerous and more wealthy than those of any other part of the county. For example, the townships north-east of York had at least double the taxable wealth of most the rest of the North Riding, and the district encompassing Howden and Hemingbrough was only exceeded in the East Riding by that of the towns of Beverley and Hull.[9] The contrast was even more striking in the West Riding, where the farmers of the Vale appear to have been far richer than those of neighbouring regions, with five to ten times the taxable wealth per acre enjoyed by the Dalesmen. Even the expanding cloth districts around Wakefield and Bradford were assessed at only half the level of the parishes in the vicinity of Selby.[10] A similar disparity existed in population density: the wapentakes bordering the western bank of the River Ouse had four to eight taxpayers per square mile, matching the five in the area of Leeds, and far surpassing the one or less found in the north-west of the Riding.[11]

A century and a half later, the population of the Vale of York had expanded greatly and grown much wealthier, reflecting a trend witnessed in most parts of the country during this period. For example, the hearth tax assessments of the 1670s suggest that the townships of this lowland region had an average of 26 households per 1,000 acres, a higher population density than Yorkshire as a whole or any of its ridings.[12] The concentration of inhabitants was especially high in the wapentakes of Howdenshire, Bulmer and Barkston Ash, all of which bordered the River Ouse (Figure 3).[13] Although by this time these areas were less densely peopled than the rapidly growing cloth districts around Leeds and Bradford, they remained much more crowded and prosperous than much of the rest of this vast county. The city of York, from which spread a web of busy highways and waterways, formed the focal point of a highly developed rural society.

Figure 3 Households per 1,000 acres in Yorkshire in 1674

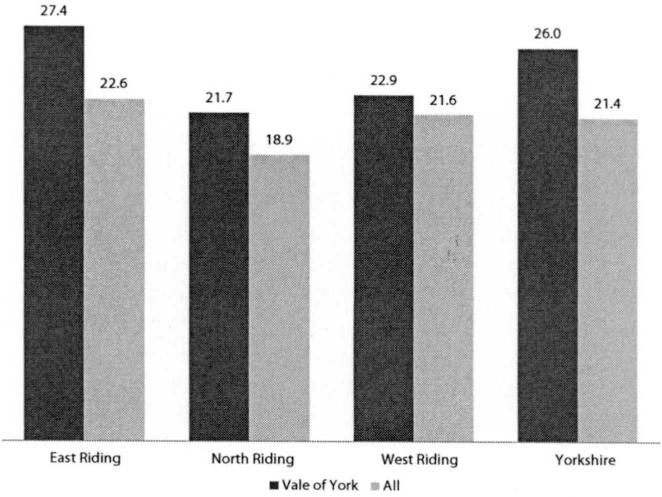

27.4

26.0

22.6

22.9

21.7

21.6

21.4

18.9

East Riding   North Riding   West Riding   Yorkshire

■ Vale of York   ▨ All

Source: See n12.

In 1801, the population of the Vale was still large and expanding. A rough estimate suggests that 170,000 to 220,000 people lived in the towns and villages of this expansive valley that stretched from Doncaster in the south to Northallerton in the north, accounting for perhaps a fifth to a quarter of Yorkshire's total population.[14] However, by this time the regional distribution of people and wealth was changing rapidly. The explosion of industry in the clothing towns of the West Riding and the commercial boom at the port of Hull were not matched by any exceptional developments in the Vale, ensuring that the lowlands – at least in relative terms – lost much of their prominence in the county's economy. That is not to say that the population stagnated or that villages sank into poverty: growth continued at a healthy rate. Indeed, some areas, such as the inland port of Selby and the increasingly drained marshlands of the Humberhead Levels, attracted immigrants and investment in the late eighteenth and early nineteenth centuries.[15] Overall, however, it is obvious that by 1800 the Vale was no longer Yorkshire's richest or most populous region. In the West Riding, for example, the Vale had a population density of about 53 people per km^2, a level that was far higher than the $12/km^2$ found in the upland district of Craven but much lower than the $192/km^2$ of the manufacturing districts of the Pennine Foothills.[16]

1.2 Social Structure

The history of the social structure of this region is even more obscure than its wealth and population, but a few observations can still be made. The work of R.B. Smith on the West Riding in the early sixteenth century provides one such window into early modern stratification. His analysis of the lay subsidy assessment of 1546 suggests that the central Vale had the highest proportion of great landlords and gentlemen of all the Riding's sub-regions at this time, but also had a below average proportion of yeoman freeholders and peasant smallholders.[17] In the 1530s, prior to the Dissolution, the land here was overwhelming held by the Church and the gentry, whereas the nobility and the Crown had considerable freeholds in other parts of the Riding.[18] Unlike the clothing districts, this area had very few rich merchants and traders, but it did have an unusually large number of taxpayers assessed on goods worth £10-£19, a group which probably consisted mostly of substantial leasehold or copyhold farmers.[19] Taken together, it seems that the Vale of Henry VIII's reign was characterised by a landed elite consisting of gentlemen and religious institutions, a broad group of tenant farmers, and of course a much larger class of labourers and cottagers, with most wealthy commoners clustered in York itself. Many of the socioeconomic features common elsewhere – crown and noble estates, dispersed manufacturing, yeoman and peasant freeholders – were largely or entirely absent.

In the late seventeenth century, when the Hearth Tax returns serve as an approximate guide to the social distribution of wealth, English society could be roughly divided into five classes (Figure 4).[20] The major landholders, represented by households taxed on ten or more hearths, accounted for less than one per cent of the families in the Vale of York. There was rarely more than one such family in each village, and many small townships had none at all. Below this layer of knights and squires were a small number of wealthy yeomen and other prosperous individuals in houses of five to nine hearths, who amounted to about four per cent of all households. Most Vale townships had at least a few of these men, though some had only one or two. Many middling yeomen occupied three or four hearths, while more modest husbandmen and craftsmen usually had two hearths. These two groups together made up around a quarter of households in the region. However, the great majority of people in every town and village lived in one-hearth homes, a group that included an extremely broad range of families. Many seem to have been well-established households with solid livelihoods. In Barlow, for example, Roger Sander, Edward Willowby, and William Watson were all assessed for only one hearth in 1672, yet they each had around ten cattle listed in their subsequent probate inventories.[21] The largest proportion probably consisted of the labourers and cottagers who made up the paid agricultural workforce required by the larger farmers, though unfortunately very little information about this group has survived. Finally, there were also a smaller number of one-hearth households who were explicitly exempted from this assessment, amounting to perhaps a quarter or a fifth of all families, and a fraction of these 'poor' households were actually paupers receiving parish relief.[22] They stood on the bottom rung of the social ladder, surviving only through a combination of hard work, luck and the kindness of neighbours.

Figure 4 Hearths per household in the Vale of York in 1674

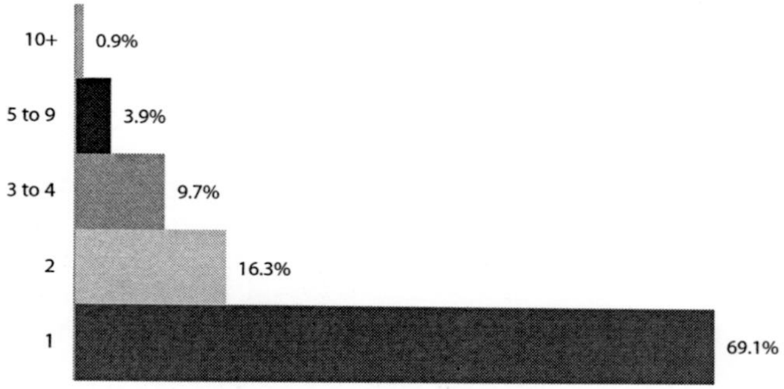

Source: See n20

The social divisions in the Vale of York at this time were not strikingly different from the rest of the county. There were, however, some discernable regional patterns.[23] In the North and East Ridings, the townships of the Vale tended to have a slightly higher number of very large, expensive houses (with the exception of marshy Howdenshire) and a much denser concentration of two or three-hearth households, but also fewer families exempted due to poverty.[24] In the West Riding, the Vale again had a higher proportion of houses with ten or more hearths but here there were also more homes of four, five or even six hearths. In addition, the lowland parishes of this Riding had fewer households with two hearths and proportionally more with only one. This suggests that the Vale as a whole, especially if the city of York were included, had a larger class of resident landholding gentry and apparently fewer poor families than the rest of the county. Yet, whereas in the northern and eastern parts of Vale there was an unusually broad layer of prosperous husbandmen and craftsmen inhabiting houses of two or three hearths, in the western villages the fortunes of some of these households had risen still further, leading to a substantial class of yeomen occupying relatively larger houses than their neighbours.

Figure 5 Agricultural occupations of fathers in the
Brayton parish register, 1698-1820

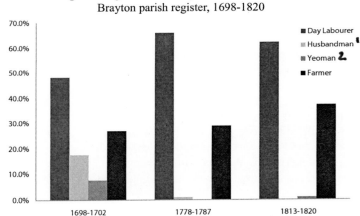

Source: BIA, PR/BRAY/3 (1698-1702), PR/BRAY/6 (1778-87), and PR/BRAY/8 (1813-20)

In the eighteenth century, a process of polarisation – accentuated by enclosure – probably created a firmer division between the increasingly affluent tenant farmers and the labourers that they employed. In the six townships of Brayton parish, for example, the baptismal register recorded an agricultural population that was shifting from a gently sloping hierarchy of 'farmers', 'yeomen', 'husbandmen' and 'day-labourers' at the beginning of the century, to a dichotomous split between 'farmers' and 'labourers' in the 1780s and 1810s (Figure 5). Moreover, like the rest of England, the Vale of York experienced an explosion of pauperism in the late eighteenth century. This region was already spending thousands of pounds per year on parish relief in 1775-76 and this increased by almost forty per cent over the subsequent decade.[25] By 1802-03, the parishes of the Vale were raising over *four times* the amount that they had been a generation earlier. Although this was less than the fivefold increase seen in Leeds, the cost of poor relief still rose slightly more than the average for the county as a whole. Overall, it seems, this region may not have had the numbers of plutocrats and paupers found in the manufacturing towns, yet the Vale was still growing more socially differentiated, with the gap between employers and employees becoming ever wider.

1.3 Livelihoods

The vast majority of people in lowland Yorkshire earned their livings through agriculture. There was little 'manufacturing' when compared to the weaving districts around Leeds or the metalworking villages around Sheffield, and no extractive industries remotely similar in scale to the lead and coal mining of the Yorkshire Dales, much less the large collieries of South Yorkshire and County Durham.[26] Instead, men and women of all social ranks drew most of their incomes directly or indirectly from exploiting the rich soils of this fertile region.

The agriculture of the Vale was chiefly 'mixed farming', combining both arable and pastoral elements throughout the early modern period, and oriented toward the market (rather than self-sufficiency) from the Tudor era onwards. The particular combination of crops and animals varied considerably across the region and over time, but certain patterns emerge clearly.

Geographical specialisation began early and was well established by the late sixteenth century. Hence, there was a greater emphasis on tillage in the drier central parts of the Vale, whereas the marshier southern parts tended to have more land devoted to pasturage.[27] In c.1540, for example, the lord's lands were mostly arable with small meadows in the manors of Hampole and Campsall on the gently undulating landscape north-west of Doncaster; in contrast, there was no arable at all, only hundreds of acres of meadow and pasture, on the demesne farm of the marshland manor of Airmyn.[28] In Barlow, a manor near Selby situated in an intermediate area between the Humberhead Levels and the central Vale, an Elizabethan inquisition post-mortem reported that the manorial estate included 40 messuages with arable holdings and around 200a. of meadow, but also contained more than 800a. of pasture.[29] Here, then, both the cultivation of corn and hay and the grazing of livestock contributed substantially to the manor's economy. In addition, the farmers of different sub-regions in the Vale already favoured different types of animal husbandry by this time. Joan Thirsk, in her broad survey of Tudor and early Stuart agriculture, suggests that the inhabitants of the western portion of the Vale specialised in cattle rearing and dairying, those of the eastern part more frequently bred horses, and those who dwelt in the Forest of Galtres sometimes kept sizeable herds of pigs.[30]

The regional propensities evident in the sixteenth century did not undergo any radical shifts in the decades that followed, though stock raising probably became more popular during the prolonged period of low corn prices that began in the mid-seventeenth century.[31] Previous work on regional variations reveals that, on average, corn and cattle were of approximately equal importance to Vale farmers in the late seventeenth century, unlike the Wolds – where corn was the chief source of income – or the rest of Yorkshire – where cattle served that purpose.[32] Sheep made up a smaller proportion of agricultural wealth here than anywhere else in the county, but work-beasts (oxen and horses) and swine were unusually common in the Vale.[33] This emphasis on 'raising cattle for their milk, meat, and hides, and upon breeding horses for coach and saddle' continued into the eighteenth century and beyond.[34]

The survival of large numbers of probate inventories from this era make it possible to examine more closely the agriculture pursued by the people of different localities. The features of particular riverside townships, for example, can be discerned through an analysis of inventories from Barlow between 1660 and 1760, combined with results of a similar analysis by Michael David Riley of inventories from Cawood, Riccall, Selby and Wistow during the same period.[35] While one might expect the farmers of these nearby villages to hold a similar balance of crops, in reality there were remarkable disparities. The chief crop in Barlow was wheat, followed closely by oats and rye, whereas in Riccall it was barley, with wheat being relatively rare. Likewise, oats were the most common crop in Wistow, found in double the number of inventories as barley, yet in the neighbouring township of Cawood there was a fairly even split between oats, barley and wheat. In addition, other food crops such as maslin, beans and peas appear in various proportions in the inventories. Thus, it seems that generalisations about even quite specific sub-regions – such as the rural settlements near Selby in the central Vale – disguise extraordinary amounts of local variation in arable cultivation.

By 1801, the date of the first attempt to survey all of England's cropland, these variations had declined substantially (Table 1). The acreage returns for the twelve West Riding parishes that bordered the Ouse show that most villages devoted a roughly similar amount of land to each major crop. Wheat was the most popular – except Nun Monkton where it was slightly exceeded by oats – and normally accounted for about thirty to forty per cent of the sown acreage. Second was oats, which made up twenty to thirty per cent, and third came pulses (principally beans) at eight to twenty per cent. Barley, potatoes, rape and turnips were found in every parish, but only rarely did any of these crops amount to more than five to ten per cent of tillage each. Other crops, such as rye, were negligible. The main axis of variation seems to be north to south, with marshlands of the lower Ouse characterised by much more extensive cultivation of potatoes but notably less barley, turnips and rape.

Table 1 Acreages of cropland for West Riding parishes along the
River Ouse in 1801

	Wheat	*Barley*	*Oats*	*Potatoes*	*Pulses*	*Turnips/Rape*
Upper Ouse	29.9%	13.7%	24.4%	1.2%	16.0%	14.4%
Middle Ouse	33.9%	10.1%	29.5%	4.5%	8.5%	10.6%
Lower Ouse	39.3%	1.9%	23.4%	19.1%	12.3%	2.8%
Average	35.1%	8.0%	27.0%	8.6%	10.7%	8.7%

Source: Michael Turner (ed.), *Home Office Acreage Returns (HO 67): List and Analysis – Part III, Staffordshire - Yorkshire, 1801* (PRO, List and Index Society, vol. 195; London, 1983), pp. 154-63

In the seventeenth and eighteenth century, the prominence of cattle in these townships is unmistakable (Table 2). It was observable even in the market towns of Selby and Cawood, and in places like Barlow owning at least one cow was nearly universal amongst yeoman, husbandmen, and even many labourers. Most farmers had five to ten beasts, a few owned herds of fifty or more, while cottagers and craftsmen usually possessed only one or two. Although stock rearing was not uncommon, cattle here were primarily employed in dairying, with over three-quarters of Barlow inventories including evidence of diary production. Some of this was for domestic consumption, but a significant number of inhabitants were clearly producing for the market – such as Clare Smith, a widow at Barlow, who despite having only five cattle also had a 'milke house' with 'a Churne', 'a cheesfatt', '2 potts with 50li of butter', 'a creame pott', 'a chees presse', '12 milk bowles', and '14 cheeses' in 1672.[36]

Table 2 Livestock in five riverside townships, 1660-1760

	Cattle	Horses	Oxen	Swine	Poultry	Sheep
Proportion of inventories						
Barlow	98%	71%	15%	56%	37%	29%
Cawood	62%	58%	5%	25%	3%	15%
Riccall	76%	52%	4%	29%	10%	11%
Selby	40%	30%	1%	18%	3%	6%
Wistow	75%	64%	5%	38%	23%	25%
Mean number of animals						
Barlow	11.5	4.9	5.4	4.2	8.1	25.4
Cawood	8.8	3.8	3.3	4.9	9.0	20.7
Riccall	5.4	3.6	3.7	2.7	5.3	20.0
Selby	4.7	3.0	4.0	3.8	5.3	38.0
Wistow	12.0	5.3	5.0	2.7	8.1	30.7
Plain of York	11.6	3.8	2.2	N/A	N/A	26.2

Sources: BIA, SELBY/WILLS (53 inventories from Barlow, 1660-1760); Riley, 'Families and their Property', p. 36 (880 inventories from Cawood, Riccall, Selby and Wistow, 1660-1760); Long, 'Regional Farming', p. 106 (for 430 inventories from 'the Plain of York', c.1690)

Horses were also extremely common, with most householders having only enough for transport and farm-work. Some farmers, especially in Wistow and Barlow, possessed studs of eight or more horses (one in ten inventories in Barlow) suggesting breeding operations, especially in the case of Thomas Sawer (d. 1671) and John Arnold (d. 1726) who each had around twenty horses.[37] As one might expect in an area with much pastoral farming, hay was grown in large quantities. It accounted for only around four per cent of probate wealth in the Vale as a whole, but was present in almost half of the inventories from Barlow.[38] Small numbers of swine, poultry, and sheep were found on many farms in these townships. Nonetheless, few men had flocks of more than ten sheep and fewer still had the forty or fifty common to upland sheep farmers. Overall, then, these other types of livestock contributed only minimally to the agrarian economy in this area. Most of the people of these villages devoted themselves to a dairy-oriented system of cattle-and-corn mixed husbandry, and only a modest number supplemented or substituted this with horse breeding or sheep farming.

Many householders whose primary livelihood came from livestock and food crops also had secondary sources of income. It is not difficult to find examples of farmers raising honeybees or cultivating rapeseed and occasionally even liquorice.[39] Likewise, disputes about tithes reveal other local agricultural products, including various combinations of apples, pears, plums, cherries, parsnips, carrots, turnips, cabbages and onions at Snaith in the 1610s, at Middlethorpe in the 1620s, and at Deighton in the 1680s.[40] Still more widespread was the growing and processing of hemp and flax. Alluvial soil was well-suited to these crops and, as a result, eighty per cent of the Barlow inventories had evidence of this in the form of 'hemp seeds', 'hemp in the hemp garth', 'undressed line' (flax), 'hemp brakes', 'line wheels', 'hemp and yarn spun', 'line yarn', or 'hemp cloth'.[41] Such goods were sometimes worth only a few shillings and never valued at more than two or three pounds, but they were still a far from negligible component in the local economy in the seventeenth and eighteenth centuries.

As befits a region crisscrossed by several large rivers, fishing was another potential source of income. In 1666, for example, John Harland of Newland, near Hemingbrough, owned not only agricultural goods but also 'one Signe Boate [and] two rowers with the nett and steding' (£2 10s.).[42] In addition, although fishing rights had declined in importance since the middle ages, they continued to be valued in the seventeenth and eighteenth centuries and were often included as part of manorial estates bordering the Ouse and the Derwent.[43] Disputes over local fisheries might even escalate into bitter, long-running conflicts, as occurred at Drax. Here the lease of 'the fishing and ferry' was yearly worth £10 and 'six rent salmons' in c.1675, but claims and counter-claims by several parties led to a legal battle and eventually violent confrontation over the course of at least eighty years beginning in about 1661.[44]

Farming and fishing were not the only ways to earn a living in the Vale. There were, of course, a wide variety of trades in the city of York and the lowland market towns, as well as local specialities such as brewing at

Tadcaster and shipbuilding at Selby.[45] Rural areas, too, had some occupational diversity. As in the rest of England, tilling a few acres of land and keeping a couple of cattle was often combined with various other employments such as blacksmithing, shoemaking, tailoring, carpentry or petty retailing. The inventory of Paul Inchbald of Barlow, who died in 1659, exemplifies the composite nature of some livelihoods.[46] He had substantial agricultural goods: 15 cattle (£29); a mare (£2 10s.); pigs and chickens (£1); sown winter corn (£5 10s.); harvested rye, wheat, barley and oats (£4 10s.); a stack of hay (£3). He also had a milkhouse with dairying equipment (£1 6s.), 30 *lbs* of butter and 12 cheeses (£1). But Inchbald augmented this with textile production: 4 stone of flax (£2); 44 yards of raw flax (£2 4s.); and 24 *lbs* of hemp yarn (10s.). And, unlike his neighbours, he possessed a workshop with shoemaking implements and 'other shopp gear' (£2) as well as 30 pairs of black shoes (£3). Most interestingly, he had a 'debt booke' listing £14 2s. 1d. owed by a dozen local debtors and one at Selby, which suggests something of the importance of neighbourhood-level trading and credit.

Table 3 Alehouses per township in Barkston Ash Wapentake in 1771

Alehouses	Townships
10+	2 (Selby, 21 alehouses; Tadcaster, 13)
5 to 9	3 (Clifford, 7; Sherburn-in-Elmet, 7; Bramham, 5)
3 to 4	7
2	11
1	14
0	4*

Note

There were also several townships not included in the list which probably possessed none.

Source: WYAS-W, QE 32/17

Often, communications within and between villages were facilitated by the innkeepers and alehousekeepers whose prevalence was extensive in the seventeenth and eighteenth centuries (Table 3). Most public houses were concentrated in market towns (Selby, Tadcaster and Sherburn) or the settlements along the Great North Road (Clifford and Braham), but there were a surprising number of entirely rural townships with two, three or even four of their own. This suggests that villages like South Milford and Carlton – with three and four alehouses respectively in 1771 – were not isolated from the prodigious concourse of traders and travellers that flowed through England long before the arrival of railways.

1.4 Local Culture

The people of the Vale of York were not especially known for having a unique local culture or worldview – they lacked the famous distinctiveness attributed to natives of Cornwall, the Fenlands or the Forest of Dean. Nonetheless, one can catch glimpses of the cultural life of this region in early modern records, and several features are worth noting. Religion was, of course, a central element in pre-industrial society, perhaps especially in Yorkshire, and the extensive research into the county's religious history undertaken by Bill Sheils and others has provided valuable insight into patterns of belief in the Vale. In the early sixteenth century, this region was well-endowed with religious institutions and showed itself to be intensely loyal to the 'old ways'. For example, most of Yorkshire's monastic houses, the wealthiest and most numerous in England, were situated in and around York and Selby or along the edges of the Dales and the North York Moors.[47] Then, when the Dissolution began in 1536, thousands from these areas raised their banners in the Pilgrimage of Grace, with especially strong and early support emerging from the villages between York and Howden.[48] Yet, whilst post-reformation Catholic congregations existed in York itself and a few places in the southern Vale such as Carlton, Hemingbrough and Howden, popular Catholicism seems to have been mostly confined to Holderness and upland Yorkshire in the late sixteenth and early seventeenth centuries.[49] Likewise, puritanism had established itself in York and its environs under the early Stuarts but was far less common in the Vale than in the industrial districts of the West Riding.[50]

There was a shift in the religious geography of the county from the mid-seventeenth century. Quakerism, for example, found adherents in York and Thirsk yet its most remarkable advances came in upland areas such as the North York Moors and Ryedale.[51] Other nonconformists, such as Presbyterians and Baptists, fared better in the Vale during the late seventeenth century only to find themselves fading away in the century that followed.[52] Instead, it was Methodism that became the most prominent and successful religious movement in this region after its emergence here in the 1750s, which resulted in a religious map in which mainstream Anglicanism primarily competed with Quakerism in the uplands and with Methodism in the lowlands.[53] In addition, Catholicism made inroads into the Vale at places like Thirsk, Northallerton and Sherburn-in-Elmet during this same period, acquiring a broader social base and becoming less dependent on gentry support.[54]

By the mid-nineteenth century, when the census of religious worship reveals patterns of attendance in exceptional detail, regional variation had become less obvious. For example, the Vale of Mowbray had one of the highest proportions of church-goers, with the Church of England and, secondarily, Wesleyan Methodism serving decent congregations, whereas the Selby registration district had unusually few church-goers, around three-fifths of whom were Methodists.[55] Topography, landholding and agricultural organisation thus appear to have been important to the religious character of Yorkshire's sub-regions in the late medieval and early modern period, but this link had broken down by the Victorian era.

Literacy and education shaped cultural life in the Vale in many of the same ways as religion did. Admittedly, in sixteenth-century Yorkshire, reading and writing would have been largely restricted to the gentry, the clergy and a small group of wealthy commoners.[56] When widespread evidence first becomes available in the mid-seventeenth century, the north of England was still 'steeped in illiteracy', but the Vale of York may have been at least a partial exception to this rule.[57] For example, in a group of settlements near Wetherby at the western edge of the Vale, a full third of testators, including over half the craftsmen, showed evidence of literacy by signing their names to their wills in 1660 to 1688.[58] The rate was roughly the same for this period in the environs of Selby during this period, improving to about fifty per cent by the end of the century and then to above seventy per cent by around 1750.[59]

The signatures or marks recorded by brides and grooms in the marriage register in the decades after the Marriage Act of 1753 provide more comprehensive data as it is less socially biased than the evidence from wills. The material collected from this source by Robert Unwin and W.P. Baker reveals the approximate levels of literacy in eight Vale parishes in the late eighteenth century (Table 4). Interestingly, geography was not a major determinant: the rate varied relatively little between parishes and the average for the Vale was only slightly higher than that for the East Riding as a whole.[60] It was also remarkably stable over time during these decades, with consistent improvements only beginning in the nineteenth century.[61] Instead, the key variables were gender and social status. Only a minority of women could sign and the same was true of grooms described as 'labourers' or 'poor', but most men had at least a minimal level of literacy and this was nearly universal amongst professionals, merchants, dealers, and victuallers.[62]

Table 4 Nuptial signature literacy in eight Vale parishes, 1754-99

Parish	Marriages	Grooms signed (%)	Brides signed (%)
Bramham	298	73.8	52.8
Hayton and Bielby	118	65.6	37.6
Hotham	82	75.0	42.8
Naburn	39	67.4	48.6
Skipwith	191	67.0	36.0
Spofforth	762	63.2	46.2
Stillingfleet	256	63.4	43.0
Thorganby	100	66.0	36.2
Total	1,846	67.7	42.9

Sources: Baker, *Parish Registers and Illiteracy*, pp. 10-11; Unwin, 'Literacy Patterns', pp. 72-78

These patterns of religious observance and educational attainment had a somewhat ambiguous place in the day-to-day culture of the Vale. Church-going, for example, was merely one aspect of the multifaceted Protestant culture of the seventeenth century, which also included many other customs and beliefs. These included an interest in supernatural 'prodigies' such as the one seen at Cawood and Wistow in 1656. Allegedly, many 'very honest men' of the district witnessed a 'Fiery Pillar' in the sky from which emerged 'a great Company of Souldiers' who battled with another vast spectral army for control of the heavens.[63] Two of the spectators here sent news of the event by letter and an account of these wondrous sights was soon published in London. This pamphlet then may have made its way north and could even have ended up in the hands of one of the supposed witnesses in Cawood or Wistow.

Indeed, the probate records from this area suggest many local gentlemen and merchants – as well as a few yeoman and craftsmen – owned books. Michael Riley has shown that over one in ten people with inventories in the vicinity of Selby possessed books between 1660 and 1710.[64] The proportion was roughly the same in the nearby township of Barlow, though the inventories sadly include very few details about the literature owned.[65] Most of the books listed were bibles and nearly all the rest were simply described by the appraisers as 'other Bookes', though John Beale also had a 'statute booke'.[66] Fortunately, the wealthy yeoman William Storr of Scalm Park in Wistow left a commonplace book that contains many hints about his reading habits in the first decades of the eighteenth century. He recorded extracts relating to topics both practical and esoteric, including medicine, astronomy, law, history and foreign countries.[67] Though some of his citations are ambiguous, it is clear that Storr read legal works, almanacs, remedy books, chronicles, travelogues and newspapers, thus showing that even a Yorkshire farmer could partake in the print culture of early modern England.

Figure 6 'We Three Loggerheads'

Source: BIA, CC/Ab/12/Caw-Wis/4/1

Finally, whilst the Vale of York undoubtedly stands out from some of the other parts of northern England due to its levels of literacy and types of religiosity, there were also plenty of hours devoted to less serious cultural activities. At Howden, for instance, Joseph Pearson reportedly allowed 'unlawfull games in his house att unlawfull tyme of the night' in February 1616.[68] Meanwhile, the bloody sport of bull bating received manorial support both here and at Selby.[69] Such rough recreations may not have appealed to everyone in this region, but they were still an essential part of its culture during this period. Even when the sturdy farmers of this district were attending to the staid business of recording the local regulations, there was apparently room for a little playfulness, for whoever recorded the customary bylaws of the manor of Wistow in the eighteenth century filled the margins with whimsical sketches of birds, fish and faces. The writer also included an old visual joke (Figure 6), venerable enough for Shakespeare to allude to it in *Twelfth Night*, that pokes fun at any who declare themselves to be a 'loggerhead' by reading the caption aloud.

Part 2. The Landscape and Its Management

The landscapes of nearly all the townships in the Vale of York shared a set of basic features. That is not to say they were uniform – in fact, there were notable variations between different parts of the Vale and ultimately each township was unique. Still, there were enough commonalities in the early modern period to make it possible to sketch a rough portrait of a typical village and its surroundings, moving outward from the settlement itself into the fields and meadows and then on to the 'marginal' land along the boundary lines and the web of infrastructure that underlay it all. As will be seen, common lands had an important and essential role in this region, and the same might be said of the long-lasting system of communal regulation that made the countryside so productive.[70] Yet, perhaps what emerges most clearly is a recognition of the fact that the landscape itself has a history – its character was neither predetermined nor permanent. Rather, it was the result of a constant effort by its inhabitants to maintain, enhance or wholly transform the environment around them.

2.1 The Settlement

At the heart of the landscape lay the cluster of buildings that made up the settlement itself. Nearly all the housing was concentrated here, unlike other parts of Yorkshire where isolated farmhouses were sometimes dispersed across many miles. Settlements in the Vale were normally linear, spread along a stretch of highway or river, or nucleated, often focused on a crossroad. This area never covered more than a tiny fraction of the land in the township even in the case of towns like Selby, with 432 houses in 1801, or substantial villages like Cawood, with 247 houses.[71]

It was here that people awoke before heading out to the fields and pastures, and it was here that they returned in the evenings to rest after finishing their daily labours. Some inhabitants, especially women and children, would have also spent many hours in or around the home during the day, doing the baking, brewing, cooking, spinning, cleaning, and mending. This was also where local craftsmen and shopkeepers plied their trades. Churches and chapels were usually located in settlements as well, so on Sundays it drew together both the devout and the sociable.

The houses themselves were small and poorly-constructed by modern standards, but they were larger and newer than those found in neighbouring regions, as is shown by the above-average number of hearths found in Vale households in the late seventeenth century.[72] Moreover, early modern probate inventories offer a glimpse inside these dwellings, and an opportunity to compare earlier structures to later ones. There were, on average, four or five rooms in a typical house in Barlow in the seventeenth and eighteenth centuries, but this figure hides the changes that occurred during that time.[73] In the 1630s, for example, John Grubb lived in a modest home with only three rooms.[74] In the main room, called 'the dwelling house', he had his dining goods including 'seaven doublers two candle sticks and one salt'. This was adjoined by 'the parlour' where he slept and 'the chamber' where he kept a wheel and loom, though these rooms were also multi-use as there was a cheese-press in the former and an extra bed in the latter. In the 1720s, the widow Ann Thompson dwelt in the same village and had a similar number of livestock, but occupied a much larger house.[75] She had a main room, a 'new parlour', an 'old parlour', three chambers, a dairy, and a bakehouse, which together contained a very substantial amount of household goods including even a clock. Such contrasts are typical of this area, where the number of rooms multiplied through the building of new houses or the expansion of old ones, and where the amount of consumer goods increased.[76]

Prior to the seventeenth century, the vast majority of these dwellings were simple timber-framed structures with thatched roofs.[77] Such houses regularly survived until the nineteenth century and these materials continued to be used for many modest new buildings throughout this period. Indeed, the importance of thatch is attested by presentments at the manor courts.

At Everingham, John Threnton, Jane Snaw and Margaret Jackson were each fined twelve pence for their houses 'lacking Thacke' in 1633, and nine tenants were fined for the same offence at Escrick in 1766.[78] However, brick made from local clays became much more popular during the early modern period, and wavy pantiles replaced many thatched roofs.[79] For instance, William Storr reports rebuilding his home, Scalm House, in 1712 for which he used 'timber, & Coles to burn bricks, & lime, & sand and bricks ... from the kilne', and he rebuilt the wagon house of brick two years later.[80] Of course the many manorial presentments for houses or chimneys being 'out of repair' indicate that not all tenants were as attentive to their dwellings.[81] Still, the popularity of rebuilding or improving housing and outbuildings is clear.[82] Churches, on the other hand, often retained the same medieval structure for centuries. For these, good freestone was normally brought from quarries at least a few miles away. The pale limestone of Tadcaster and Monk Fryston, for example, was carted or floated to York, Selby and elsewhere in the Vale.[83] However, even religious buildings rarely survived the early modern period entirely unchanged and new chapels – such as the one recorded at Barlow in 1716 – were frequently constructed from bricks.[84]

2.2 Gardens, Crofts and 'Old Inclosures'

Attached to each of the houses that stood along the main street were the little enclosed plots and yards variously called 'crofts', 'gardens', 'garths' and 'folds'. These were rarely more than an acre in size, together amounting to perhaps only a hundredth of the total land in the township. Nonetheless, they had an important role in the household's economy. Family members, especially wives and children, passed many an hour digging in the garden and attending to the pigs or poultry, for these small patches of land provided vegetables, eggs, poultry and pork. They also supplied space for growing cash crops such as fruit or liquorice and for cultivating hemp or flax to be used in domestic production.[85]

Beyond the crofts and gardens were the village's 'old inclosures', which might be used for either arable or pasture. Sometimes they were very close to the settlement, once part of large open fields, and in other places they were at the edge of the township, formed from tracts of manorial 'waste' appropriated for private use. Very few villages had no closes at all, yet they might be negligible in size. For example, the two closes mentioned at Newton-upon-Ouse before the first major attempt at enclosure in 1758 amounted to merely four or five acres.[86] Likewise, several small enclosures had been made at

Acomb by the seventeenth century, but none seems to have encompassed more than a dozen acres prior to 1770s.[87] At Skelton, the 'ancient inclosed lands' amounted to 157*a*. in 1807, only about six per cent of the township's acreage.[88] However, there were other places with much larger enclosures: Gate Fulford had an 'Old Inclosure' of about 350*a*. and a scattering of smaller ones; Cawood and Wistow had numerous closes together totalling over 4,000*a*. and covering more than half of the landscape.[89] There were also a few villages that had been entirely enclosed by the eighteenth century, such as Beningbrough which was wholly owned by the resident Bourchier family.[90] The amount of land managed 'in severalty' thus varied dramatically between localities. Nonetheless, there was a tendency nearly everywhere for these areas to expand over time. Piece by piece, closes multiplied over the years, probably accounting for the majority of land in the Vale by the mid-eighteenth century.[91]

2.3 Common Fields

When a Tudor husbandman stepped out of his house and passed through the little croft or garth behind the dwelling to reach the gate at its end, he would usually find himself looking across an open expanse known as the 'town fields'. Three, four or five fields, each of perhaps 100 to 200 acres, spread outward over the land of the township. They consisted of innumerable thin strips belonging to separate occupiers, but the strips were divided only by furrow marks and each field was managed communally rather than individually. In the summer, they were a sea of grain stretching into the distance and then, after the harvest, the gates were opened and the village livestock were herded in to graze.

Although not all townships in the early modern Vale of York had common fields, exceptions were very unusual at the beginning of this period. At least three-quarters of the townships along the River Ouse definitely had early modern 'town fields', and most of the others were small hamlets whose fields may have been subsumed within those of their larger neighbours (Table 5).[92] Yet, compared to the extremely extensive open-field agriculture found in some other areas – including much of the Midlands[93] – this region had a relatively modest quantity of unenclosed tillage. Indeed, a considerable amount of enclosure was underway or had already been completed by this period. In some cases, townships had lost all of their arable commons well before the era of parliamentary enclosure began in the mid-eighteenth century. The fields of Selby, Barlow, and Gribthorpe, for example, had been enclosed by the early seventeenth century, and those of Clifton were still important in 1618 but were then enclosed sometime before 1764.[94] There were also some townships where only a patchwork of small common fields survived amongst large numbers of closes. This was the situation in places such as Drax, Cliffe, Naburn, and East Cottingwith.[95] Finally, however, there were a number of settlements that retained very substantial open-field systems into the late eighteenth century or beyond. These included Acomb, Bishopthorpe and Asselby, where over four-fifths of the total acreage was managed communally before parliamentary enclosure, and also Holme-on-Spalding-Moor, which continued to grow most of its crops on three large town fields until the 1770s.[96] So, it seems that some arable common land survived in most townships in the Vale until at least the eighteenth century, even if it accounted for only a minority of the total cropland in some of these places by this time.

Table 5 Common fields along the River Ouse

	No.	%
1550-1750		
Settlements with no evidence of common fields	13	25
Settlements with common fields	39	75
Post-1750		
Settlements with no evidence of common fields	23	43
Settlements with common fields	30	57
minimal fields	14	47
moderate or substantial fields	10	33
extent of fields unknown	6	20

Sources: see n91

The residents of these many villages with common fields devoted a considerable amount of energy to protecting and sustaining this shared resource, and this policing was nearly always conducted through the manor courts. They had two primary objectives: managing access and preventing damage. Access to the common fields was probably the more important of these two concerns. Of course, only tenants of the manor were to have use of the fields, while sub-tenants and non-residents were normally excluded. Hence, the long list of bylaws passed by the jurors of Escrick in October 1753 included one forbidding any inhabitant from pasturing livestock on the town fields unless they had 'good right' to do so.[97] Locals often attempted to block outsiders from even indirect access by, for example, fining tenants 'for taking into the field other peoples sheep to winter' at Hemingbrough in 1715.[98] Timing was obviously an important restriction on access as well. It was only after the harvest had been completed, during the season described by a Wistow custumal as 'the time of eatage or averish', that animals were permitted in the open fields.[99] Likewise, gleaning was only permitted after the stacks had been taken in.[100] Manorial jurors thus regularly presented individuals whose horses, cattle, swine or sheep were found unlawfully grazing in these areas. Peter Russome, amerced 12*d.* at Drax in 1627 'for his horses trespassinge in Newland field', was just one of many who were punished for such offences throughout the period.[101]

Protecting the fields from the damage that could be caused by negligence or misuse was the other main priority. This aspect of local management was essential if the value of the land was to be maintained. The manorial records of Bishopthorpe, stretching across the seventeenth and eighteenth centuries, provide examples of some of the most common regulations of this type. Jurors here demanded that every man with holdings in the common fields to 'diligently looke & weed his corn land in due and convenient tymes & season', and that no one risk harming the crop by attempting to 'drive any louse beasts through Bishopthorpe Southfield'.[102] They also punished individuals for specific acts of neglect and abuse, such as fining Margaret Teasdale 6*d.* for leaving 'her backfront gate into the field open', which would have allowed livestock to wander in, and fining William Robison 6*s.* 8*d.* 'for ploughing the Comon baulk away in the far South field'.[103] However, in Bishopthorpe and elsewhere, the most frequent point of contention was the maintenance of the drainage required to keep the common fields from becoming waterlogged and of the fences necessary to protect them from unlawful grazing. Hence, there were endless presentments for insufficient dikes at the land ends in the North Field or along the Far South Field, insufficient fences against the Hard Corn Field, or between the Barley Field, the Fallow Field and the Common, and so forth.[104] So, although the land itself was privately owned and the crops belonged to particular individuals, communities policed their town fields throughout the year, imposing penalties for a wide range of offences in order to sustain this vital resource.

2.4 Meadows and Ings

If an early modern husbandman, instead of walking towards the town fields, made his way to the bank of the nearest river, he would soon be standing in the alluvial meadows known as 'the Ings'. These common meadowlands, like the open fields, produced both private profits (an annual crop of hay) and collective benefits (a rich post-harvest pasture). Nearly all of the riverside townships in the Vale of York – at least those north of the fens and marshes of the Humberhead Levels – possessed a strip of ings, which they usually grazed in common.[105] The seasonal flooding experienced by these lands provided a fertile layer of silt that made them exceptionally valuable. In some townships, only the old closes nearest the settlement were worth more per acre.[106]

Common meadows, with rare exceptions, covered less of the landscape than the village's town fields. Those enclosed in the late eighteenth century included both small ings at Gate Fulford (54*a*.) and Stillingfleet (76*a*.) as well as large ings at Cawood (288*a*.) and Wistow (151*a*.).[107] Sometimes they were enclosed over the course of the seventeenth century, as seems to have happened to the Common Ings (over 100*a*.) at Barlow. In most cases, however, they continued to be collectively managed until the coming of parliamentary enclosure and occasionally long after. For example, the South Ings at Acaster Malbis (113*a*.) continued to be communally pastured even in the early twentieth century.[108]

Controlling access was always a key priority. The long-running court books of the manor of Acaster Malbis show this process at work. According to an Elizabethan bylaw, for example, no horses or cattle were permitted in the South Ings after Whitsunday, and any livestock found there would cost their owners a fine of 12*d*. per animal.[109] Over three centuries later, in 1907, the manor's 'Byelaws and Rules for the Regulation of the South Ings' continued to address these issues. They ordered that no stock was to be let onto the Ings unless possessed by the owner at least 14 days, and also set the stint for grazing on the 'fog' (the nourishing grass that sprang up after the hay harvest) according to each tenants acreage.[110] Other communities laid down restrictions on access by non-residents, such as the prohibition passed by Linton-on-Ouse in 1745 against letting grass in the Ings (or other commons) to any 'outer town person' for a month after the fog.[111] Furthermore, individual attempts to quietly appropriate and enclose parts of the Ings were vigorously resisted at Wistow in the late sixteenth century, because even a minor encroachment would have denied the manorial tenants access to part of their common right.[112] Unsurprisingly, however, the most frequently presented offence concerning access to the meadows was for 'trespassing' livestock, grazing 'without right' or at unlawful times.[113]

Maintaining the value of common ings required additional regulations. Damaging the hay by making a pathway 'over the Carr Ings for either foot or hors in time of middew' was forbidden, and negligent acts such as 'leaving the Inges yard open' were also liable to penalties.[114] Individuals who failed to repair the fences that shielded meadows from wandering livestock often received fines from the manor court, just as they did in the case of common fields, but greatest concern seems to have been associated with preventing these lands from being overwhelmed with water. At Brotherton in the 1660s, for instance, the jurors ordered that every man should keep a sufficient fence against the Ings, but also should fill any breaches in the banks that protected the meadowland from river floods.[115] There were also numerous orders to scour ditches, 'grip' lands and maintain 'gotes' on the Ings in order to keep them reasonably well-drained.[116] Indeed, even in the midst of enclosure manorial jurors continued to impose bylaws to this effect. So, two years after the passage of an Act of Parliament in 1806 to enclose the open meadows at Kelfield, the jury commanded that the 'main drain in the Ings [was] to be completed of the width directed by the Commissioners Award'.[117] All of these measures were designed to prevent destructive incidents like that which unfolded at Barlow in 1636, when Peter Halliday was fined 10s. for 'drowning the common Inges'.[118]

2.5 Woodlands, Marshes and Pastures

Villagers seeking the least-peopled part of the landscape could head out from the compact row of houses and gardens, cross the surrounding fields and meadows, and step into one of the sizeable swathes of woodland or 'wastes'. These were normally found at the edge of the township, often running along the boundaries and serving to help separate a village from its neighbours. In some parts of the Vale, such as the Humberhead Levels around Howden and Goole, there were very large tracts of marshland that provided not only grazing but also fish, fowl, turves and rushes.[119] In the slightly drier (but still low-lying) districts around York and Selby, the commons were smaller and often provided whins (furze), underwood or timber in addition to pastureland.[120]

Overall, however, there were few townships in lowland Yorkshire with open lands comparable to the huge shared moors found in other parts of northern England.[121]

Woodlands, especially communally managed ones, were relatively scarce in this region.[122] There was nearly 500a. of shared woodland in Escrick in around 1600, and just over 200a. in Sutton on Derwent when it was enclosed in 1777.[123] However, of the 52 townships along the Ouse, only Cawood and Wistow had substantial commonable woods listed in their parliamentary enclosure awards.[124] These two settlements shared five Haggs, consisting of almost 1,000a. in 1641, and additional Outwoods.[125] Here, the tenants defended their rights of access from repeated attempts at lordly enclosure. The custom, as described in both the 1560s and the 1700s, was that the lord of the manor could temporarily fence two of the haggs for seven years after making a 'wood fall' but then had to re-open them to common for the tenants' cattle and pannage for their swine.[126] Such guarantees of access were mirrored by the restrictions on outsiders like those made in 1753 at Escrick where only inhabitants with 'good right' were allowed to put stock in the common wood, on pain of a steep fine of £1 19s.[127] Likewise, jurors here set limits on the amount of fuel that could be collected, declaring that tenants could only 'fell or kid any Common wood' for a month in the spring and only within their 'stint' which was three loads per messuage and two loads per cottage.[128] Private woods, often in the form of parks, were equally rare and obviously had less impact on local society. Tracts like Naburn's Great Wood (80a.) and Barlow Hagg (128a.) might provide pasture for their owners and employment for gamekeepers, but they never had a prominent place in the rural landscape.[129]

Other commons – including marshes, carrs and unspecified 'pastures' – were much more prevalent than woodlands. In fact, they appear to have been nearly universal, with almost every Vale of York township possessing such lands until the late eighteenth century.[130] They accounted for upwards of forty per cent of the surface area in Howdenshire, where the adjoined lands of Bishopsoil and Wallingfen amounted to nearly 9,000a. in the late eighteenth century and were shared between thirty different settlements.[131] Likewise, at Reedness and Swinefleet on the southern banks of the Ouse, around 3,200a. of marshy common pasture covered more than half the acreage of these two townships.[132] However, in most settlements along the Ouse north of its junction with the Aire, such commons accounted for between a tenth and a third of the surface area at the time of their enclosure.[133]

These commons may have been on ill-drained marginal land, but they contributed to the rural economy by providing pasturage, fuel, building material and much else, so villagers predictably invested time and expense in policing them carefully. Pasture was only to be enjoyed by residents and even they could not over-stock the grounds with unreasonable numbers of animals. Hence, inhabitants of Thorpe in Balne were ordered to not 'gist any strangers Cattell upon Thorpe Marsh', and those of Selby were prohibited from putting more 'goods' upon the common than they could winter.[134] Similarly, manorial jurors developed a wide array of rules to govern the collection and extraction of valuable resources from these 'wastes'. At Deighton in 1584, they commanded that 'none but tenantes of the lorde of this manor shall digg any turfe on the Common', imposing a heavy fine (6s. 8d.) for disobedience.[135] A few miles away, at Acomb, the jury not only repeatedly restricted the collection of turves on the moor to two loads per messuage and one per cottage, they also equally limited the cutting of whins.[136] This prevented the moor from being depleted by the ruthless stripping of resources for sale outside the township. One can see the danger inherent in the possibility of unconstrained commercial exploitation of commons in the pains laid at Selby in the late seventeenth century: the growing shipping trade led to a ban on taking earth for ballast from East Common, and the demands of the pottery industry meant that potters had to pay an annual fee of 2s. 6d. for the privilege of digging clay on the common and even then only within the bounds marked out by the freehold jury.[137]

Communities also sought to protect their commons from damaging negligence by imposing rules similar to those made concerning fields and meadows. Bylaws against putting 'scabbed' or diseased horses in the shared pastures were very widespread, and at Brotherton only stallions of suitable height were allowed to mix with the rest of the town herd on the marsh.[138] These efforts to preserve the health and quality of grazing livestock were augmented by close monitoring of the state of the fencing around the commons, both to keep lawful animals in and to keep unlawful ones out.[139] The state of the land itself was also an issue that received attention. Spoiling the common marsh by carrying loads of wood and coals across it to the river, or by leaving obstructions on it, was thus punished repeatedly by the Brotherton jurors in the late seventeenth and early eighteenth century.[140] And, of course, maintaining at least some drainage was essential or else the commons might end up like those shared by Camblesforth and Barlow in 1729, when they were described as 'very much oppressed & damaged with water'.[141]

2.6 Infrastructure

Between, around and through all of these various parts of the landscape ran the shared 'infrastructure' essential to local life. This included a wide range of key features such as roads, paths, bridges, waterways, drainage works, embankments, hedges, fences, gates, stiles, and village pinfolds. Their functions were manifold and their utility immeasurable. Some elements – for example, most roadways – were legally part of the common land of the manor in the same way as 'wastes' and marshes, whilst others – including many fences and ditches between closes – were supposed to be entirely private property.[142] Yet, as will be seen, the 'private' status of the latter did not deter communities from regulating them when they felt that the public good was at stake. So, although local infrastructure accounted for little acreage and much of it was completely held in private hands, its central role in the success of the Vale's economy ensured that it was usually subject to vigilant collective oversight.

Major roadways between cities and market towns served as the vital arteries and veins of the trading networks that distributed agricultural produce and a growing variety of consumer goods. As such, these routes fell under the purview of county magistrates, who sought to keep them in a reasonable state of repair either by punishing parishes that failed to maintain them or by providing subsidies from the county rates.[143] This began to change later in the period with the establishment of turnpikes, but in most cases the traditional system remained in place until at least the late eighteenth century.

Smaller roads and tracks – the capillaries of regional economic circulation – were normally managed by the authority of the manor courts, and this continued long after turnpikes began appearing.[144] Quantitatively, pains and presentments related to transport routes made up around eight per cent of the total over the whole period, appearing in nearly all substantial sets of regulations.[145] The manorial jurors demanded that individuals maintain the 'highways' adjoining their lands and the streets fronting their doors, as well as calling on all inhabitants to attend the 'common days work' prescribed by statute for repairing shared roads.[146] Similar rules applied to minor bridges and foot-stiles.[147] On occasion, common resources might be made available for these tasks, as at Wistow where the lord customarily assigned sufficient 'Bowes ... for mending of the high Wayes'.[148] Ultimately, however, keeping travel and transport links open necessitated regularly punishing offenders for obstructing them with rubbish, carrion and overhanging trees, or for encroaching on them with sandpits, ploughland and other infringements.[149]

The emphasis placed on preserving customary routes can also be seen in the bylaw at Ryther against 'stopp[ing] the hye wayes that hath bin used and accustomed within this xx^tie yeares unlese yt be for saveing of Corne & as suffitient a waye being left', and the demand laid on John Woodall of Wistow to permit passage through Potter Yard, which was 'an ancient highe way for fout foalkes'.[150]

Waterways formed another indispensable part of the local, national and international transportation infrastructure. Navigable rivers were normally supposed to be open to all, but they were subject to various different (and sometimes competing) authorities, including the Crown and urban corporations.[151] The City of York, for example, had been granted control over most of the Ouse and it sometimes used its authority to force villagers downstream to remove obstructions, such as fishgarths.[152] Nonetheless, local communities occasionally used their manor courts to police access to these important 'highways'.[153] At Selby, for example, from at least the early seventeenth century, the jurors regulated the use of the Lord's Staithes and sought to prevent individuals from blocking them with lumber or boats.[154] Meanwhile, at Thorpe in Balne, the town kept a 'Common Boat' which the jurors forbade anyone from taking from 'the Landing place' for longer than two hours at a time.[155]

Managing and monitoring boundaries was, it seems, an aspect of local regulation that was even more important than maintaining roadways. Fences, hedges and walls demarcated different owners, occupiers and land uses as well as protecting crops from wandering animals. To that end, manorial juries in the Vale of York passed dozens of bylaws and presented hundreds of individuals for related offences, around one in seven (fourteen per cent) of the total recorded in the sample.[156] At the Easter court at Acomb in 1555, for example, twenty-five men and women were fined for not repairing their fences, and at the Easter court in 1707 another twenty-four were fined for like misdemeanours.[157] Hedge-breaking, which was punished at Howden, Bishopthorpe, and many other places, similarly threatened the integrity of local boundaries, though it was also considered to be equivalent to theft as it was usually an attempt to illicitly collect fuel to warm a cold hearth.[158] But focusing solely on firm barriers of this sort would ignore the fact that unfenced boundaries were policed too. Manorial, parochial and civil perambulations exemplified this facet of communal regulation. The most famous was the annual riding of the bounds of York, a procession that circumnavigated the extensive 'average grounds' outside the city walls in which the citizens enjoyed common pasturage rights until 1826.[159] Less grand were those that took place in small settlements like Barlow, where eighteenth-century perambulations helped to fix in the tenants' minds the unmarked division between their common and that of the township of Camblesforth.[160]

Finally, a ubiquitous and complex grid of drains and flood defences in lowland Yorkshire made possible the relatively high level of agricultural productivity enjoyed by this region.[161] To describe it as merely an important part of the rural landscape would be an understatement, for it was perhaps the most critical component in the whole system of infrastructure. Some indication of its centrality can be gleaned from the remarkable number of words, including several particular to local dialects, used to describe the various parts of this system – not just dikes, ditches and embankments, but also 'gotes', 'runners', 'descenders', 'grips' and 'dreiners'. The Commissions of Sewers for the West and East Ridings policed some aspects of the drainage system in several places in southern Yorkshire in the seventeenth century, but this issue was primarily managed by individual localities.[162] Indeed, it received a very large proportion of the regulatory energy of the manor courts, accounting for over a quarter (twenty-eight per cent) of the pains and presentments recorded in the sample.[163] These overwhelmingly consisted of banal but necessary orders to scour clogged dikes or remove obstructions from drains, and it was not unusual for ten or fifteen such presentments to be made at a single meeting of the court.[164] By end of the period, sometimes this had become the only offence handled by the manor, as at Everingham between 1790 and 1857.[165] Related problems also arose, though in smaller numbers. At Wistow, for example, one finds tenants with holdings in the North Field ordered to 'gripp' their lands there in 1662, and three people – including a gentleman – fined 39s. per rood for insufficient banks against the Ouse in 1688.[166] It was also the custom here to supply manorial timber for making and repairing 'clows' (outfall sluices with floodgates) and other 'common' infrastructure.[167] Such efforts were simply unavoidable in townships like Long Drax, where an observer in 1758 lamented that much of the land 'so low that it would be overflowed by every little flood, nay, I believe I may say, by the highest spring-tides, if not prevented by the height of strong banks'.[168] As a whole, then, the web of highways, footpaths, river landings, fences, hedges, drains and banks that stretched across the Vale of York cannot be ignored when attempting to understand the history of the landscape in the region. They were just as fundamental to local society as the houses, fields and pastures around them.

Conclusions

Taking a step back from the minutiae of individual townships, several features of the early modern Vale of York become apparent: the region's distinctive place in northern England; the impact of local regulation on the landscape; and, the changing nature of the world inhabited by ordinary people. By the sixteenth century, this was a region that had already stood out from its neighbours for many generations. In Roman Britain, the Vale – with Eboracum at its centre – had formed the heartland of the northern territories, and it retained this role throughout the middle ages and into the early modern period. This history, combined with the Vale's extensive waterways and fertile farmland, gave it a character that was very different from many of its neighbours. Whereas many northern districts were thinly populated uplands, this low-lying area seldom had more than a few miles of open space between its numerous, compact settlements. Similarly, there was a sharp contrast between the countless northerners whose modest livelihoods came from sheep-farming, cloth-working or mining, and the Vale dwellers whose heightened prosperity was build on a system of mixed agriculture that produced immense quantities of corn, beef, milk, cheese and horses. The regional culture was influenced by these traits and, although any suggestions on this subject must be very tentative, the region was perhaps more literate and religiously orthodox than nearby areas that lacked the Vale's well-established class of gentry and 'substantial inhabitants'. This was, then, a place far removed from the caricature of the poor, barren, backward 'North'.[169]

The fruitful landscape that made this society distinctive did not simply emerge fully formed from Mother Nature's womb. While topography formed the foundation for much of what followed, the lowland countryside was as much the product of human endeavour as woollens of Leeds or the cutlery of Hallamshire. Every part of a township – from the houses and gardens at its centre to the marshy pastures at its margins – required regular attention from residents and remained subject to some degree of collective oversight. This policing operated primarily through the authority of the manor courts and, until mid-eighteenth century, higher levels of government only rarely intervened. Thus, not only was Walter King right to argue that early Stuart courts leet were 'still needful and useful', these institutions often remained essential to local agricultural life until the era of parliamentary enclosure.[170] Moreover, this management involved more than just regulating commonable land. It also entailed keeping a close watch over the shared infrastructure of the rural economy – encompassing transportation networks, local boundaries, and drainage systems. It would be easy to dismiss the resulting innumerable minor acts of enforcement as mundane, and indeed they normally were, yet they fulfilled an indispensible function, without which agrarian life would very quickly begin to disintegrate. Hence, manorial regulation contributed to the relative wealth and stability of this part of England by protecting against the degradation of shared land and resources, punishing over-use or negligence of these 'commons', linking locals to both internal and external markets, dividing townships into countless different specialised fields and farms, and – perhaps most importantly – preventing villagers' livelihoods from simply washing away in one of the region's recurring great floods.

Not only did the early modern landscape of the Vale of York experience constant maintenance and management by its inhabitants, it also underwent several major changes thanks to repeated human intervention, which in turn influenced the nature of rural society itself. All of the social and economic features of this region noted at the beginning of this section – its dense population, its material wealth, its high productivity – were present under the Tudors and indeed before. Yet, in each case, they increased over the years that followed. Over the course of the seventeenth and eighteenth centuries, the number of inhabitants multiplied several times, houses expanded in size and quality, consumer goods became more available than ever, and agricultural yields grew gradually larger. However, these advances were accompanied by an increasingly 'privatised' landscape and, eventually, the decline of local collective management. In the sixteenth century, almost every settlement seems to have had some form of common land. By mid-eighteenth century, however, the proportion had declined somewhat and the remaining commons had often been reduced in size. Still, this process should not be exaggerated. This was a region characterised by a substantial and gradually increasing quantity of 'closes', but also one that featured many town fields – especially in the drier areas – and plentiful numbers of marshy common pastures, which could cover thousands of acres in places like Howdenshire. It was only during the era of parliamentary enclosure, beginning in about 1740, that common rights were finally extinguished. This was also the period in which many communities ceased to manage their landscapes through the manorial courts. Instead, authority was either shifted upward to higher levels of government or downward to individual owners. By the time railways began unfurling themselves across the rich, flat farmland in the 1830s, the Vale of York had changed in ways that would have been unimaginable to an Elizabethan villager.

Notes

1 Cited in R.W. Unwin, 'Tradition and Transition: Market Towns of the Vale of York, 1660-1830', *Northern History*, 17 (1981) p. 72.

2 Baron F. Duckham, *The Yorkshire Ouse: The History of River Navigation* (Newton Abbot, 1967) ch. 2-4; Unwin, 'Tradition and Transition'.

3 Countryside Commission, *Countryside Character* (8 vols; Cheltenham , 2006) vol. 3, pp. 32-6.

4 *Ibid.* vol. 3, pp. 53-7. Note that my impression from early modern sources is that the River Aire (rather than the Escrick Moraine) formed the southern boundary of the central Vale, thus including Selby here rather than in the Humberhead Levels.

5 *Ibid.* vol. 3, pp. 101-6.

6 David Hey highlights this diversity in his *A History of Yorkshire: 'County of Broad Acres'* (Lancaster, 2005) pp. 1-2, 5.

7 For the geographical distribution of 'cattle and corn' districts see Joan Thirsk, 'The Farming Regions of England', in *idem.* (ed.), *The Agrarian History of England and Wales* (hereafter *AHEW*) (8 vols, London, 1967-2000) vol. 4, p. 4; Joan Thirsk, 'Introduction', in *idem.*, *AHEW* vol. 5, pt. 1, pp. xx-xxi.

8 Sixteenth century figures largely accord with regional distribution suggested by the poll tax returns of the late fourteenth century: Jeremy Goldberg, 'Population and Settlement in the Later Middle Ages', in Robin A. Butlin (ed.), *Historical Atlas of North Yorkshire* (Otley, 2003) pp. 96, 98; R.B. Smith, *Land and Politics in the England of Henry VIII: The West Riding of Yorkshire: 1530-46* (Oxford, 1970) pp. 28-33.

9 John Sheail (edited by R.W. Hoyle), *The Regional Distribution of Wealth in England as Indicated by in the 1524/5 Lay Subsidy Returns* (2 vols, London, 1998) vol. 1, pp. 186, 190.

10 *Ibid.* p. 195.

11 *Ibid.* p. 194.

12 David Hey *et al.* (eds), *Yorkshire West Riding Hearth Tax Assessment: Lady Day 1672* (London, 2007); J.D. Purdy, *Yorkshire Hearth Tax Returns* (Hull, 1991). Calculations based on the wapentakes of the Ainsty, Barkston Ash, Osgoldcross, Ouse and Derwent, Howdenshire, Allertonshire, Birdforth, Bulmer, Gilling East, and the city of York. If York is excluded, the figure is still 22.9 households per 1000*a*. Acreages taken from *Census: Abstract of Answers and Returns* (1831).

13 Their household densities were respectively 50%, 29%, and 22% higher than those of their Ridings.

14 Estimate derived from the wapentake population figures in *Census: Abstract of Answers and Returns: Enumeration* (1801), with range necessary due to several wapentakes (Birdforth, Claro, Strafforth and Tickhill) including both upland and lowland townships.

15 The number of baptisms in Howdenshire rose by 32% between 1750 and 1800 (from 149 to 196), those of Barkston Ash wapentake (which included Selby) rose by 63% (from 266 to 434) over the same period: *Census: Abstract of the Answers and Returns: Parish Registers* (1801) pp. 353, 366.

16 For population density and change from 1851 to 1901 in the modern county of North Yorkshire, see Richard Lawton, 'Population Change, 1700-1900', in Butlin, *Historical Atlas*, pp. 123-6.

17 Smith, *Land and Politics*, pp. 109-18, esp. 110 (Table XII).

18 *Ibid.* p. 75 (Table VI)

19 *Ibid.* pp. 109-118.

20 All data from Hey *et al.*, *West Riding Hearth Tax*; Purdy, *Yorkshire Hearth Tax*. See also Michael David Riley, 'Families and Their Property in Early Modern England: A Study of Four Communities on the Yorkshire Ouse, 1660-1760 (York Univ. PhD thesis 1990) pp. 104-5.

21 Borthwick Institute for Archives at the University of York (hereafter BIA), SELBY/WILLS (Roger Sander, inventory, 22 December 1674; Edward Willowby, inventory, 8 November 1677; William Watson, inventory, 4 June 1672).

22 Note that these poor households were systematically undercounted in the hearth tax returns, especially in the West Riding, which means that the nominal figures for both one-hearth households and total households must be inflated to take account of this.

23 All data from Hey *et al.*, *West Riding Hearth Tax*; Purdy, *Yorkshire Hearth Tax*.

24 My calculations accord with assessment offered by Bill Sheils, 'Hearth Tax Returns', in Butlin, *Historical Atlas*, pp. 113-15.

25 Calculations based on wapentake-level figures in *Poor Law: Abstract of the Answers and Returns* (1804) pp. 585-656.

26 E. Lipson, *The History of the Woollen and Worsted Industries* (London, 1921); David Hey, *The Fiery Blades of Hallamshire: Sheffield and Its Neighbourhood, 1660-1740* (Leicester and New York, 1991); Butlin, *Historical Atlas*, ch. 9.

27 Joan Thirsk, 'Yorkshire and Lincolnshire', in *idem.*, *AHEW*, vol. 4, pp. 33, 35.

28 Smith, *Land and Politics*, pp. 16-17

29 The National Archives (hereafter TNA), WARD 7/20/126.

30 Thirsk, 'Yorkshire and Lincolnshire', pp. 33, 37.

31 P.J. Bowden, 'Agricultural Prices, Wages, Farm Profits and Rents', in Thirsk, *AHEW*, vol. 5, pt. 2, pp. 1-118.

32 W. Harwood Long, 'Regional Farming in Seventeenth-Century Yorkshire', *Agricultural History Review*, 8 (1960), p. 105.

33 *Ibid.* pp. 105-107.

34 David Hey, 'Yorkshire and Lancashire', in Thirsk, *AHEW*, vol. 5, pt. 1, pp. 71-3, 78-81.

35 All data from BIA, SELBY/WILLS; Riley, 'Families and their Property', ch. 1. See also Long, 'Regional Farming'.

36 BIA, Selby/Wills (Clare Smith of Barlow, inventory, 2 July 1672). For large-scale butter production in the most northern part of the Vale up to Yarm, see Hey, 'Yorkshire and Lancashire', in Thirsk, *AHEW*, vol. 5, pt. 1, p. 73; North Yorkshire County Record Office (hereafter NYCRO), QSB 1685/33; 1686/31-35, 46, 50, 97-98, 186; 1690/16; 1692/199, 356, 392; 1694/92-104; and *passim*.

37 BIA, SELBY/WILLS (Thomas Sawer, inventory, 24 March 1671; John Arnold, inventory, 14 December 1726.

38 For the average for the Vale, see Long, 'Regional Farming', p. 105.

39   See, respectively, BIA, SELBY/WILLS (Thomas Messinger, inventory, 27 March 1662; Thomas Sawer, inventory, 24 March 1671; Jane Holmes, inventory, n.d. [1667]). Likewise, in 1697, Pontefract 'full of great Gardens walled in all round, ... which is mostly intended [for] the increasing of Liquorish, which the Gardens are all filled with, and any body that has but a little ground improve it for the produce of Liquorish': Christopher Morris (ed.), *The Illustrated Journeys of Celia Fiennes, 1685-c.1712* (Stroud, 1995) p. 103.

40   BIA, CP/H/4837; CP/H/2091; CP/H/4114; CP/H/4419.

41   Unfortunately there are no comparable figures for the other four townships as Riley appears to have only recorded hemp and flax as sown crops. He finds less than 5% of inventories with these crops in Cawood and Selby, around 20% in Wistow, and around 30% in Riccall: Riley, 'Families and their Property', pp. 42-43. For the growing of hemp in Howdenshire in the 1570s, Snaith in the 1610s and Escrick in the 1640s, see BIA, CP/G/2442; CP/H/4837; CP/H/38/97.

42   BIA, SELBY/WILLS (inventory of John Harland, 5 June 1666).

43   TNA, WARD 7/20/126; West Yorkshire Archive Service at Wakefield (hereafter WYAS-W), QE 13/3/1 (1789, 1790); K.J. Allison (ed.), *A History of the County of York: East Riding* (hereafter *VCH: ER*) (London, 1976) vol. 3, pp. 15, 33, 41, 59, 64, 80, 109, 163, 177. For medieval fishing see Duckham, *Ouse*, pp. 34-37.

44   Hull History Centre (hereafter HHC), U DDEV/31/245-254. For fishing at Drax in the 1510s, see BIA, CP/G/226.

45   Butlin, *Historical Atlas*, pp. 163, 186-8, 196-7.

46   BIA, SELBY/WILLS (Paul Inchbald, inventory, 10 February 1659).

47   Bill Sheils, 'The Dissolution of the Monasteries', in Butlin, *Historical Atlas*, pp. 106-7.

48   *Ibid.* p. 108; Smith, *Land and Politics*, ch. 5; Michael Bush, *The Pilgrimage of Grace: A Study of the Rebel Armies of October 1536* (Manchester and New York, 1996) ch. 3.

49   Bill Sheils, 'Roman Catholic Recusancy, 1580-1792', in Butlin, *Historical Atlas*, pp. 109-10; Hugh Aveling, *Post-Reformation Catholicism in East Yorkshire, 1558-1790* (York, 1960) pp. 35-6.

50   John Anthony Newton, 'Puritanism in the Diocese of York (excluding Nottinghamshire), 1603-1640' (London Univ. PhD thesis 1955) pp. 21, 56-8; Ronald A. Marchant, *The Puritans and the Church Courts in the Diocese of York, 1560-1642* (London, 1960) pp. 74-96, 208-10; Bill Sheils, 'Post-Restoration Nonconformity and Dissent', in Butlin, *Historical Atlas*, p. 116. For Lollardy and early Protestantism, which was concentrated in York and other large towns see A.G. Dickens, *Lollards and Protestants in the Diocese of York, 1509-1558* (London, 1959) pp. 246-7.

51   Sheils, 'Post-Restoration Nonconformity and Dissent', pp. 116, 118.

52   Ibid.

53   Ibid.

54   Sheils, 'Roman Catholic Recusancy', pp. 110-111.

55   Bill Shiels and Richard Lawton, 'The Religious Census of 1851', pp. 137-9.

56   No statistics from this period have yet been collected for Yorkshire, but it was probably broadly comparable to the Diocese of Durham: David Cressy, *Literacy and the Social Order: Reading and Writing in Tudor and Stuart England* (Cambridge, 1980) pp. 120, 142-63.

57 *Ibid.* pp. 75, 201. Unfortunately Cressy's figure of 26% for signature literacy in Yorkshire in 1641-44 is based on only two parishes (Pontefract and Cherry Burton), neither of which were in the Vale.

58 Robert Unwin, 'Literacy Patterns in Rural Communities in the Vale of York, 1660-1840', pp. 68-72.

59 Riley, 'Families and Their Property', p. 120.

60 Averages for the sample of 17 East Riding parishes were 65.0% for grooms and 40.2% for brides in 1754-1800: W. P. Baker, *Parish Registers and Illiteracy in East Yorkshire* (York, 1961) p. 12.

61 Averages for the Vale parishes were 68.4% for grooms and 43.4% for brides in 1754-59, almost identical to the averages for the period as whole.

62 For rates by occupation, see Unwin, 'Literacy Patterns', pp.74-8.

63 Anon., *A True Relation of Strange and Wonderful Sights seen in the Air ... at Wistoe ... [and] at Cawood* (London, 1656) pp. 1, 4-5.

64 Riley, 'Families and their Property', p. 122.

65 Six of the 37 inventories (16%) for Barlow from 1650 to 1699 included books.

66 BIA, SELBY/WILLS (inventory of John Beale, n.d. [1670s]).

67 BIA, MD 112. For more about Storr and his book, see Riley, 'Families and their Property', pp. 128-32; W. Consitt Boulter, 'The Book of Remarks of William Storr, of Scalm Park, 1678-1731', *York Archaeological Journal*, 7 (1881) pp. 44-62. For the recorded reading of a later, more elite resident of the Vale see Helen Kirk (ed.), *'Ye dear Object of my Affections': The Diary of William Lockwood of Easinwold, 1778-1836, From 1st of January 1796 to 30th September 1797* (Easingwold, 1996) pp. 55-56.

68 TNA, SC 2/211/61.

69 *Ibid.*; HHC, U DDLO/21/171, 172.

70 For other studies of the post-medieval regulation of commons in England, see Martina De Moor, Leigh Shaw-Taylor and Paul Warde (eds), *The Management of Common Land in North West Europe, c. 1500-1850* (Turnhout, 2002); Angus Winchester, *The Harvest of the Hills: Rural Life in Northern England and the Scottish Borders, 1400-1700* (Edinburgh, 2000).

71 *Census: Abstract of Answers and Returns: Enumeration* (1801) p. 434.

72 *Ibid.* p. 11.

73 Mode of 4 and mean of 5.1 for 54 inventories with usable room data, 1637-1799: BIA, SELBY/WILLS.

74 BIA, SELBY/WILLS (inventory of John Grubb, 21 July 1638).

75 BIA, SELBY/WILLS (inventory of Ann Thompson 21 May 1722).

76 For nearby townships see Riley, 'Families and their Property', pp. 106-12.

77 Alison C. Armstrong, 'Vernacular Building Materials', in Butlin, *Historical Atlas*, pp. 218-19.

78 HHC, U DDEV/10/31; HHC, U DDFA/2/2/16.

79 Armstrong, 'Vernacular Building Materials', in Butlin, *Historical Atlas*.

80 BIA, MD 112.

81 For examples, see TNA, SC 2/211/61 (Howden, estreats, 9 April 1616; Skelton, estreats, 1 October 1616); HHC, U DDBH/3/2 (Deighton, pains, 25 October 1638); BIA, Ware 7 (Hemingbrough, presentments, 30 September 1684, 25 October 1705, etc.).

82 In 1799 it was reported that, around Selby, '[f]arm houses and offices are well enough constructed, but very improperly situated, as they are mostly in villages': Robert Brown, *General View of the Agriculture of the West Riding of Yorkshire* (Edinbrough, 1799) p. 42.

83 Armstrong, 'Vernacular Building Materials', p. 219; Stephen Moorhouse, 'Medieval Yorkshire: A Rural Landscape for the Future', in T.G. Manby, S. Moorhouse, and Patrick Ottaway (eds), *The Archaeology of Yorkshire: An Assessment at the Beginning of the 21st Century* (Leeds, 2003) p. 194.

84 BIA, Terrier B, Brayton (1716).

85 *Ibid.* p. 16.

86 Stanley Price and George Ruffhead, *Three Yorkshire Villages: Historical Studies of Beningbrough, Linton-on-Ouse and Newton-on-Ouse* (Newton-on-Ouse, 1973) p. 56.

87 Harold Richardson (ed.), *Court Rolls of the Manor of Acomb* (2 vols. Leeds, 1969, 1978), vol. 1, pp. 90, 101, 156-7, 167, 178, 201, 210, 226, 246; vol. 2, pp. 292-3; Barbara English, *Yorkshire Enclosure Awards* (Hull, 1985) p. 2.

88 NYCRO, MIC 307.

89 Yorkshire Archaeological Society Archives, DD 88/8 (Gate Fulford enclosure award, plan, 1807); NYCRO, CRONT 1148 (Cawood and Wistow enclosure award, 1780, copy).

90 Price and Ruffhead, *Three Yorkshire Villages*, p. 44;

91 Around 34% of the acreage in the 52 riverside townships was enclosed by parliamentary enclosure between 1746 and 1882, to which one must add some late piecemeal enclosure and some twentieth-century commons, suggesting perhaps 50 to 60% had been enclosed by c.1750.

92 Totals of settlements with common fields should be regarded as minima as these figures are primarily determined by a *lack* of contradictory evidence. In addition to manorial records and enclosure awards (too numerous to be listed here), evidence has been drawn from English, *Yorkshire Enclosure Awards*; Roger J.P. Kain, John Chapman, and Richard R. Oliver (eds), *The Enclosure Maps of England and Wales, 1595-1918* (Cambridge, 2004) [http://hds.essex.ac.uk/em/, last accessed 10 November 2011]; P.M. Tillott (ed.), *A History of the County of York: The City of York* (hereafter *VCH: York*) (Victoria County Histories, 1961) pp. 498-506; Allison (ed.), *VCH: ER*, vol. 3; M.W. Beresford, 'Glebe Terriers and Open Field, Yorkshire', *Yorkshire Archaeological Journal*, 37 (1948-51) pp. 323-68. All figures should be regarded as approximate at best given the inexact nature of the surviving evidence.

93 Thirsk 'The Farming Regions of England', in *idem.* (ed.), *AHEW*, vol. 4, pp. 5-7; Oliver Rackham, *The History of the Countryside: The Classic History of Britain's Landscape, Flora and Fauna* (London, 2000) pp. 3-5, 164-79.

94 For Selby and Barlow, this conclusion is based on an examination of probate material and manorial papers from c.1540-1800. For Gribthorpe, see Alan Harris, *The Rural Landscape of the East Riding of Yorkshire, 1700-1850: A Study in Historical Geography* (Oxford, 1961) p. 54. For Clifton see Tillott (ed.), *VCH: York*, p. 499n30; English, *Yorkshire Enclosure Awards*, p. 33.

95 English, *Yorkshire Enclosure Awards*, p. 41; Allison, *VCH: ER*, vol. 3, pp. 59, 79; Harris, *Rural Landscape*, p. 54 .

96 English, *Yorkshire Enclosure Awards*, pp. 2, 8, 18; Harris, *Rural Landscape*, p. 54.

97 BIA, PR/ESC 20.

98 BIA, Ware 7 (presentments, 13 May 1715).

99 BIA, CC/Ab/12/Caw-Wis/4/1.

100 BIA, Rev IV (Bishopthorpe, pains and presentments, 4 May 1625).

101 HHC, U DDEV/32/6. Unfortunately, they rarely state whether the 'trespass' was due to pasturing out of season or pasturing 'without right'.

102 BIA, Rev IV (pains and presentments, 4 May 1625).

103 Ibid. (presentments, 21 October 1702, 14 November 1756).

104 BIA, Ware 7 (Hemingbrough, presentments, 24 April 1676, 16 October 1690, 25 October 1705); BIA, Rev IV (Bishopthorpe, presentments, 18 November 1715, 24 October 1735, 14 November 1756), and *passim*. Ditches and dikes were doubly important because they could also serve as fence-like barriers.

105 Of the 32 townships on the Ouse above the Rivers Aire and Derwent only three (Newton-on-Ouse, Selby, and Newland) did not have Ings. For sources n91 and A.H. Smith (ed.), *The Place-Names of the West Riding of Yorkshire* (8 vols. Cambridge, 1961-1963). Moreover, some townships without river access, such as Skipwith, also had ings: Allison, *VCH: ER*, vol. 3, p. 96.

106 Alan Harris, *The Open Fields of East Yorkshire* (York, 1959) pp. 11-12; *idem.*, *Rural Landscape*, p. 116.

107 Allison, *VCH: ER*, vol. 3, pp. 32, 107; NYCRO, CRONT 1148.

108 YMA, Hailstone BB13 (Barlow, presentments, 7 October 1636); BIA, SELBY/WILLS (Richard Heminlay, inventory, 12 September. 1695); BIA, Wenlock 7/7 (Acaster Malbis, by-laws, 1907).

109 NYCRO, ZDV(F) (pains, 3 April 1573)

110 BIA, Wenlock 7/7. Specifically, they ordered the Fog to be agisted as follows: horse over two years, 2*a*. 2*r*.; horse under two years, 1*a*.; mare and foal, 2*a*.; cattle over two years, 1*a*.; cattle over one year, 3*r*.; cattle under one year, 2*r*.; five sheep, 1*a*.

111 West Yorkshire Archive Service at Bradford (hereafter WYAS-B), DB10/C2.

112 BIA, CC/Ab/12/Caw-Wis/4/1.

113 See, for example, presentments for calves, sheep, oxen, and horses in the Ings at Everingham: HHC, U DDEV/10/31 (presentments, 23 October 1633, 8 April 1634, and 27 October 1634); or the presentments for over-grazing in the Ings at Acomb in 1624: Richardson , *Acomb*, vol. 1, pp. 140-1.

114 BIA, PR/ESC 20 (Escrick, pains, 25 October 1753); YMA, Hailstone BB13 (Barlow, presentments, 6 Oct 1636).

115 NYCRO, ZEC (Brotherton, pains, 16 April 1667, presentments, 25 Oct 1675).

116 HHC, U DDBH/3/2 (Deighton, pains, October 1585); BIA, PR/ESC 20 (Escrick, pains, 25 October 1753); NYCRO, ZDV(F), unsorted (Acaster Malbis, pains, 2 October 1606).

117 HHC, U DDPR/8/3.

118 YMA, Hailstone BB13.

119 Briony McDonagh, 'Preparatory Report on Volume X: Howden and Howdenshire' (unpublished paper for Victoria County History, 2007); Thirsk, 'The Farming Regions of England', in *idem.*, *AHEW*, vol. 4, pp. 35-6; Harris, *Rural Landscape*, pp. 50-2. See also the common pastures and moors of Reedness and Swinefleet (around 3200*a.*) enclosed in 1760 and 1801: English, *Yorkshire Enclosure Awards*, p. 115.

120 Harris, *Rural Landscape*, pp. 50-2. See also the records from Acomb, Barlow, Deighton, Escrick, and Everingham cited below.

121 Winchester, *Harvest of the Hills*, esp. ch. 2.

122 Ian Dormor, 'Ancient Woodland', in Butlin, *Historical Atlas*, pp. 215-18. The main exception to this was the Forest of Galtres, between York and Easingwold, which may have included about 7,600*a.* of woodland in 1630; however, it was disafforested at this time and there were substantial encroachments on these wooded areas in subsequent decades: Geoffrey C. Cowling, *The History of Easingwold and the Forest of Galtres* (Huddersfield, 1967) pp. 175-190. By the nineteenth century, the former forest had been reduced to a few, small scattered woods.

123 Allison, *VCH: ER*, vol. 3, pp. 23, 177.

124 Of course some unspecified 'commons and wastes' mentioned in the awards would have included lightly-wooded pasture, but this was probably not extensive.

125 BIA, CC/Ab/8/5.

126 HHC, DDBH/19/33-34; BIA, CC/Ab/12/Caw-Wis/4/1; BIA, MD 112, p. 38.

127 BIA, PR/ESC 20.

128 However, 'thorns [were] to be feld when thear is occation for them': *Ibid.*

129 Allison, *VCH: ER*, vol. 3, p. 79; TNA, E 134/2Jas2/Mich36; BIA, TA335.S.

130 Of the 52 townships along the Yorkshire Ouse, only two do not have any obvious evidence of commons in the early modern period. These are Beningbrough and Airmyn, both of which were dominated by a single landholder from at least the sixteenth century. Closer investigation may reveal that they too had commons.

131 McDonagh, 'Howden and Howdenshire', pp. 5-6, 23.

132 English, *Yorkshire Enclosure Awards*, p. 115.

133 This estimate is based on a sample of enclosure awards from eighteen townships. The average proportion devoted to 'common' (excluding common fields) was 22%.

134 Doncaster Archives (hereafter DA), DD/DC/A2/2 (Thorpe in Balne, bylaws, 1669); HHC, U DDLO/2/8/3 (Selby, presentments, 26 April 1716).

135 HHC, U DDBH/3/2.

136 Richardson, *Acomb*, vol. 1, pp. 24, 29-32, 37, 46, 59-60, 88, 91, 105, 109-10 (presentments and pains, 1567-1602).

137 HHC, U DDLO/21/171-172 (7 October 1669 and 25 April 1682).

138 For examples of the former, see Richardson, *Acomb*, vol. 1, p. 9 (pains, 6 May 1555); NYCRO, ZFR (Burton Salmon, pains, 1659); DA, DD/DC/A2/2 (Thorpe in Balne, bylaws, 1669); BIA, Ware 7 (Hemingbrough, presentments, 13 May 1715); York City Archives, Acc. 135, N.P. 1/1 (Nether Poppleton, presentments, 1750); BIA, PR/ESC 20 (Escrick, pains, 1753). For the latter, see NYCRO, ZEC (Brotherton, pains, 1667).

139 BIA, Rev VIII (Wistow, pains, 1 Oct 1662); DA, DD/DC/A2/2 (Thorpe in Balne, bylaws, 1669).

140 NYCRO, ZEC (Brotherton, 1667-1729).

141 HHC, U DDEV/64/29.

142 Rackham, *Countryside*, p. 279.

143 For examples from Vale townships in the 1670s and 80s, see WYAS-W, QS1/15/4/8/4; QS1/19/5/8/20;   QS1/19/8/8/8;   QS1/20/6/6/18;   QS1/19/3/6/19;   QS1/20/4/1/32; QS1/20/6/8/4.

144 Christopher Jessell, *The Law of the Manor* (Chichester, 1998) pp. 103-8.

145 For details see Appendix 1. Note that this figure includes those related to bridges, stiles, and river-landings, which made up c.1% of the total.

146 For examples of the former see HHC, U DDEV/32/6 (Drax, presentments, 1627); BIA, Ware 7 (Hemingbrough, presentments, 1691, 1699, 1700); HHC, U DDLO/2/8/3 (Selby, October 1709); NYCRO, ZEC (Brotherton, 1729). For examples of the latter see HHC, U DDBH/3/2 (Deighton, 1587); YMA, Hailstone BB13 (Barlow, 1636); NYCRO, ZFR (Burton Salmon, pains, 1659); DD/DC/A1/5/1-27 (Owsten, presentments, 1709, 1722); HHC, U DDBH/14/2 (Ryther, pains, n.d.).

147 BIA, Rev IV (Bishopthorpe, pains, 1617, presentments, 1765, 1774, 1795, 1805); BIA, Rev VIII (Wistow, pains, 1 October 1662); HHC, U DDLO/2/8/3 (Selby, presentments, 6 May 1702).

148 BIA, CC/Ab/12/Caw-Wis/4/1.

149 For examples of the former see TNA, SC 2/211/61(Howden, 1 October 1616); NYCRO, ZFR (Burton Salmon, pains, 1659); HHC, U DDEV/32/6 (Drax, presentments, 1660); DA, DD/DC/A2/2 (Thorpe in Balne, presentments, 1784). For the latter see HHC, U DDEV/10/31(Everingham, 8 April 1634); HHC, U DDLO/1/15 (Barlow, October 1638); BIA, Ware 7 (Hemingbrough, presentments, 18 April 1700).

150 HHC, U DDBH/14/2 (Ryther, pains, n.d.); BIA, Rev VIII (Wistow, pains, 1 October 1662).

151 Humphrey William Woolrych, *A Treatise of the Law of Waters* (Philadelphia, 1853) pp. 29-30, 62-7.

152 Duckham, *Yorkshire Ouse*, pp. 29, 34-8.

153 Jessell, *Law of the Manor*, pp. 111-13.

154 HHC, SE/CR/28 (pains, 26 April 1625); HHC, U DDLO/2/8/3 (presentments, 6 May 1702).

155 DA, DD/DC/A2/2 (byelaws, 1669).

156 See Appendix 1.

157 Richardson, *Acomb*, vol. 1, pp. 8-9, 190.

158 TNA, SC 2/211/61 (Howden, 9 April 1616); BIA, Rev IV (Bishopthorpe, presentments, 21 October 1702).

159 Tillott, *VCH: York*, p. 501.

160 East Riding of Yorkshire Archives and Local Studies Service, DDCL/124. The Manorial Documents Register at TNA indicates that records of manorial perambulations also survive for other Vale settlements such as Skelton, Wressle, and Tadcaster. For more on the significance of this practice see Steve Hindle, 'Beating the Bounds of the Parish: Order, Memory and Identity in the English Local Community, c.1500-1700', in Michael J. Halvorson and Karen E. Spierling (eds), *Defining Community in Early Modern Europe* (Aldershot, 2008) pp. 205-27.

161 Describing the area around Selby in 1799, it was noted that 'Strict attention is necessary in keeping the ditches clean, and letting the water off the fields, which are greatly hurt by rain water stagnating upon them': Brown, *Agriculture of the West Riding*, p. 42.

162 DA, DX/BAX/65159/1; June Sheppard, *The Draining of the Marshlands of South Holderness and the Vale of York* (York, 1966) pp. 13-27.

163 See Appendix 1.

164 For examples of large groups of presentments of this sort, see HHC, U DDBH/3/2 (Deighton, October 1585); HHC, U DDEV/32/6 (Drax, presentments, 29 April 1628 and 24 April 1661); BIA, Ware 7 (Hemingbrough, 24 April 1676); WYAS-B, DB10/C2 (Linton-on-Ouse, pains and presentments, 12 March 1745).

165 HHC, U DDEV/10/31; HHC, U DDEV/22/6.

166 BIA, Rev VIII.

167 BIA, CC/Ab/12/Caw-Wis/4/1.

168 John Burton, *Monasticon Eboracense, and the Ecclesiastical History of Yorkshire* (York, 1758) p. 100.

169 For early modern perceptions of 'the North' see Helen M. Jewell, *The North-South Divide: The Origins of Northern Consciousness in England* (Manchester, 1994) ch. 5.

170 W.J. King, 'Early Stuart Courts Leet: Still Needful and Useful', *Histoire sociale / Social History*, 23 (1990) pp. 271-99.

Appendix 1. Quantifying Manorial Regulation

Offence	c.1550-1649 (45 sets)		1650-1749 (56 sets)		1750-c.1850 (30 sets)		c.1550-c.1850 (131 sets)	
	No	%	No	%	No	%	No	%
Unlawful grazing	158	19.0	253	23.7	52	10.1	463	19.2
Drainage and embankment	174	20.9	232	21.8	243	47.2	649	26.9
Roads, paths, stiles and bridges	66	7.9	93	8.7	38	7.4	197	8.2
Fences and hedges	103	12.4	185	17.4	43	8.3	331	13.7
Unlawful appropriation	74	8.9	35	3.3	8	1.6	117	4.8
Risks and nuisances	39	4.7	52	4.9	8	1.6	99	4.1
Houses and chimneys	11	1.3	5	0.5	45	8.7	61	2.5
Sub-tenants and vagrants	41	4.9	33	3.1	2	0.4	76	3.1
Retailing and crafts	42	5.0	8	0.8	1	0.2	51	2.1
Assaults and affrays	19	2.3	7	0.7	0	0.0	26	1.1
Other	106	12.7	163	15.3	75	14.6	344	14.3
Total	833	100.0	1,066	100.0	515	100.0	2,414	100.0

Note

The sample excludes procedural rules and offences, fines related to inheritance or property transfers, appearing at court, and officers keeping their accounts. Although most of the categories are self-explanatory, it should be noted that 'Unlawful Appropriation' includes encroaching on common lands, hedge-breaking, and unlawfully or excessively taking soil, sand, whins, turves, underwood or timber.

Sources: Acaster Malbis, 1561-1907 (NYCRO, ZDV(F); BIA, Wenlock 7/7); Acaster Selby, 1647-1673 (John Goodchild Collection, ACASTER MANOR); Acomb with Holgate, 1544-1822 (Richardson (ed.), Acomb); Barlow, 1636-1638 (YMA, Hailstone BB13; HHC, U DDLO/1/15); Bishopthorpe, 1617-1811 (BIA, Rev IV); Blacktoft with Scalby, 1616 (TNA, SC 2/211/61); Brayton, 1657 (HHC, U DDLO/11/2); Brotherton, 1667-1721 (NYCRO, ZEC); Burton Salmon, 1659 (NYCRO, ZFR); Deighton, 1585-1638 (HHC, U DDBH/3/2); Drax, 1628-1717 (HHC, U DDEV/32/6); Escrick, 1753-1766 (BIA, PR/ESC 20; HHC, U DDFA/2/2/16); Everingham with Thorpe, 1633-1857 (HHC, U DDEV/10/31; HHC, U DDEV/22/6); Fulford, 1694-1854 (YAS, DD 88/1); Hemingbrough, 1675-1836 (BIA, Ware 7; BIA, Ware 14/3); Howden, 1616 (TNA, SC 2/211/61); Kelfield, 1808 (HHC, U DDPR/8/3); Kilpin, 1616 (TNA, SC 2/211/61); Linton-on-Ouse, 1745-1750 (WYAS-B, DB10/C2); Nether Poppleton, 1746-1750 (YCA, Acc. 135, NP/1/1); Riccall, 1601-1705 (YAS, MD 106); Saltmarsh, 1616 (TNA, SC 2/211/61); Selby, 1540-1727 (HHC, U DDLO/21/170-172; HHC, SE/CR/28-29,46; HHC, U DDLO/2/8/3); Skelton, 1616 (TNA, SC 2/211/61); Thorpe Willoughby, 1657-1658 (HHC, U DDLO/11/2); Wistow, 1662-1688 (BIA, Rev VIII; BIA, CC.Ab/12/Caw-Wis/4/1).

Appendix 2. Illustrative Documents

The three transcriptions that follow are intended to provide examples of the sorts of regulations described in the preceding section. Whilst each manor is unique, with its own particular combination of local rules, these three sets are relatively typical of the other Vale manors during their respective periods. For a transcription of all of the surviving court rolls of a single manor from the sixteenth to the nineteenth century, see those of Acomb edited by Harold Richardson. The editorial method adopted is as follows: contractions and abbreviations have been extended silently; spelling, capitalisation and punctuation have been retained except that names have been capitalised; difficult or obscure words have been explained in the body of the text in square brackets.

Manor of Barlow, Pains and Presentments, October 1639

HHC, U DDLO/1/15

This roughly drafted document consists of four full pages and one fragment and includes a total of 29 items as well as a list of 13 jurors. Most are pains, but these are intermixed with several presentments. Although the first page is dated October 1638, the other pages appear to date from a court held at Easter, probably in 1638 or 1639. The regulations covered a range of offences. Orders concerning dikes and fences were the most frequently occurring. Transportation links also repeatedly received attention, as in the presentments for disobeying the statute for a 'Common work' day, when roads were collectively repaired. Other regulations were attempts to protect crops by demanding the ringing of swine and to protect other resources by punishing wood-stealing, hedge-breaking and encroaching on the common. The only pain that was somewhat unusual was the order for the miller to keep weights and scales at his mill – this was presumably a customary expectation but was not mentioned in the other manors in the sample. It should be noted that the lords of the manor – Sir Henry Cholmley and Dame Catherine Twistleton – resided at Barlow at this time and owned nearly all of the land, which may have made the appeal of manorial regulation slightly stronger here. However, it also appears that the township's arable land had been enclosed, making field ordinances unnecessary.

October paines laide by the Jury whose names ar under written 1638

[1.] Imprimis a paine layde that every one make thaire brigges [bridges] and steels [stiles] betwixt neighbor and neighbor betwixt this and Candlemas day – every default – vid

[2.] Item a paine laide that every one that be taken breaking heges or beare any green wood – every default – xiid

[3.] Item wee lie a paine that every one keepe thaire swine suffetiently rung and so keep thame every default – iid

[4.] Item wee lie a paine that John Richeson the millner keepe weights and scales at his millne betwixt and Christmas in paine of – vis viid

[5.] wee lie an paine that Grace Man make hir fence betwext hir and Elizabeth Grub betwixt and Martinmas next in pane of everie defall – xiid

[6.] a paine laide that the water sure [sewer] be suffitient scourd from the bond ing gate to the Seuell Hills and so to the river of Owse in pane of everie rowd undon – xiid

***

[7.] Item a paine layde that Richard Johnson mak suffetient fence betwixt his Moslay Mouth Close and Henry Benetland close betwixt and may day in paine of every rowd undun – iiis iiiid

[8.] Item a paine layde that Richard Johnson dike the same Close side to the Mo[o]re in pane of every rowd undun – iiis iiiid

[9.] Item a paine layd that the same from the Stor Gate to the Marsh Bridg be suffetiently scourd betwixt and Michellmas in pane of every rowd undun – vid

[10.] Item A paine layd that Sandird Canell be suffitiently diked from the towne side to the Car Dike in paine of euery rowd undun betwixt and Whitsuntide – iiis iiiid

[11.] Wee finde that Thomas Seale of Brayton is dead since the last Court, and that Thomas Seale is his sone, and heire and is above the age of xxity yeares, And holdeth diuers frehoull Lands of the Lord of this Manor, And payeth the yearly fre rent of iiis iid

[12.] We present James Clay for Carreing wood – xiid

[13.] Wee present John Richardson for not keeping scales and weights at his mill – vis viijd

[14.] We present Georg Nutte for leauing the out wood gate open Cumming and goeing and letting our goods wrong – iiis iiiid

[15.] We present Henry Halleday for incroching of the Lords ground – xiid

[16.] We present Georg Nutte for incroching of the Lords ground – vid

[17.] We present John Motlay And Edward Lunslay for not being at the Common work – iiis iiiid

[18.] We present William Scafe for the like – iiis iiiid

[19.] We present George Nutte for the like – iiis iiiid

***

[20.] We present Robert Marshall for defects we finde in the Bellecroft dike – iis

[21.] Item a paine layd that Thomas Knight take his wood out of Robert Clay dike by the Out Wood Laine betwixt and whitsuntide in the paine of default – xxxixs

[22.] Item a payne layde that John Larbut take his wood out of William Sander dike and William Ette betwixt and Whitsuntid in paine of defalt – xxxixs

[23.] Item a paine layd that the dreaner [drain] from Christopher Clay Calfe House to the March Gate be suffetcent Diked betwixt and Bartholmu next in paine of ever[y] rowd undun – iiid

[24.] Item a pane layd that Elizabeth Grub dike the West Laine Close dike from hir gate to moslaymouth gatestock Betwixt and Whitsuntide in pane of every rowd undun – iiid

[25.] Item a paine layed that no man take any earth from Henry Bennetland Moslay Mouth Close gate to the spoylling of his Way to the sayd close in paine of the defallt of every lode – iiis iiiid

[26.] a pane layd that none make a way thro to William Jackson close and Thomas Warde Stor Close adioyning at the end of it in pane of every default – xiid

[27.] a pane layd that William Scafe dike his dike suffetiently betwixt Robert Clay Baske Close and William Scaffe spring betwixt and Whitsuntid next in payne of every rode undun – iiis viiid

***

[28.] A payne laid that none drive any goods through Wykrofte [*damaged*] in carte or carriage before Michaelmas in paine of every default – iii [*damaged*]

[29.] A payne layd that every one keepe the hywayes in the Huntingleys and Wykrofte a foote and with draughts in paine of every default – iiis [*damaged*]

***

Manor court jurors

Joannes Seule
Willielmus Jackson
Thomas Noble
Thomas Seale
Willielmus Fisher
Joannes Bramham
Willielmus Ettie
Thomas Beale
Henricus Benitland
Richardus Bell
Thomas Messenger
Willielmus Saunder
Joannes Smyth

Manor of Hemingbrough, presentments, 14 October 1686
BIA, Ware 7

This is a single page of 24 presentments and list of 13 jurors. It concludes with a few rough (and partly illegible) procedural notes. Eight of the presentments are procedural fines for not attending the previous court. Of the remaining offences, the largest proportion are cases of tenants (including two gentlemen) not maintaining dikes, embankments and fences. The attempts to protect crops from unyoked swine and an improperly tethered horse were typical of early modern manor courts, but the complaints against hedge-breakers are unusual to find in late seventeenth-century regulations. Rarer still is the presentment of two men (including the bailiff) for a bloody affray, as these were normally handled by quarter sessions by around 1600. The manor was held by the Ingrams of Temple Newsam, but there the land was divided into a variety of smaller freeholds and copyholds. There were some enclosed parcels, but townfields and other substantial common land survived until parliamentary enclosure in 1844. It was only then that the manorial jury ceased to punish offences.

Hemingbrough the 14th October 1686
Presentments maide by the Jury as followeth:

[1.] Imprimis Thomas Williamson for his Cunstable Close dike being not suficently dicked – 1s 0d

[2.] Hanna Foster for her oke trese [oak trees] in the Burn Close being not cut according to paine – 1s 0d

[3.] John Robinson Gentleman for thre Harthstone land ends not being dicked – 0s 3d

[4.] Francis Bacon Gentleman for two Harthstone land ends not being dicked – 0s 2d

[5.] Henry Bayles Gentleman for one land end in the Motlecroft being not sufficiently bannked – 1s 0d

[6.] Francis Bacon Gentleman for one land in the Motlecroft being not suficently fenced – 0s 1d

[7.] Thomas Maslin for two land ends in the Twendickes being not dicked – 0s 2d

[8.] George Rose for one swine being not Runge – 0s 2d

[9.] Ann Hartley for one swine being not runge – 0s 2d

[10.] George Rose for his children breaking hedges – 1s 8d

[11.] Ann Hartley for her sone breaking hedges – 1s 8d

[12.] Elias Robinson for his Children breaking hedges – 1s 8d

[13.] Anthony Bayne for his Children breaking hedges – 1s 8d

[14.] John Robinson balife for his Children breaking hedges – 1s 8d

[15.] John Robinson balife and Abraham Hartley for a blood and fraye – 3s 4d

[16.] Robert Coggrane for one hors being Tethered Contrary to paine – 0s 2d

for not appearing at the Court held the 22 April

[17.] Thomas Fanks Gentleman – 0s 2d

[18.] Sara Atkinson – 0s 2d

[19.] Robart Brooke – 0s 2d

[20.] Thomas Maslin – 0s 2d

[21.] Edward Robinson – 0s 2d

[22.] John Coggrane – 0s 2d
[23.] William Orry – 0s 2d
[24.] Thomas Picocke – 0s 2d

The Juryers Hands

William Barratt
John Barrett
Robert Coggrane
Francis Bacon
Ralph Bray
William Breard
William Phillips
Robert Bentley
John Geysdall
Thomas Pottage
Mathew Hollins
Robert Newitt
Hanrill Ellitt

William Barrett }
Francis Bacon   } Jur. [?officers]

We Confirme these presentments
William Barratt
Francis Bacon

presentments [*illegible*] Cur. tent. 14th die Oct. 1686
[*illegible*]

Manor of Fulford, presentments, 7 December 1781

YAS, DD/88/1
This entry from Fulford's court book includes 11 regulatory presentments
in addition to several procedural fines and a jury list. As was usual, the jury
was sworn in October and then the verdict was presented a few months later.
The number and range of offences condemned was relatively small. Broken
fences were the primary concern. The only other presentments related to

'insufficient' bridges and blocked watercourses. The limited purview of the court's regulations was mainly a result of the enclosure of the township's open-fields, meadows, and moor in 1759. Nonetheless, the manorial jury here continued to make presentments of this sort into the 1850s. From 1763, the manors of both Gate and Water Fulford were held by the Key family, who also had perhaps six hundred acres of land here.

Manor of Fulforth }   To wit / The View of Frank pledge with the Court Leet and Court Baron of Mrs Katherine Key Lady of the said Manor held at the House of George Wilkinson within the Manor the Nineth day of October one thousand Seven hundred and Eighty one Before George Townend Gentleman Steward of the said Court.

The names of the Jury

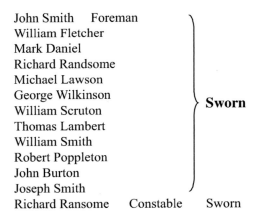

John Smith   Foreman
William Fletcher
Mark Daniel
Richard Randsome
Michael Lawson
George Wilkinson
William Scruton   **Sworn**
Thomas Lambert
William Smith
Robert Poppleton
John Burton
Joseph Smith
Richard Ransome   Constable   Sworn

[*list of payments for 'fealty' and for 'suit and service'*]

Verdict day on Friday the 7th day of December.

At this Court the Jury presented
[1.]   Mr. Bridges for the West end of his closes being undone – 2s 6d
[2.]   John Hessay for his Ings Close being undone – 2s 0d
[3.]   Mr. Barstow for the West End of his Close being undone – 3s 0d
[4.]   Mr. Milburn for his Bridge being Insufficient – 1s 0d
[5.]   Henry Taylor for the North End of his Close being undone – 1s 6d

[6.]   William Tuke John Joy John Dale Widow Chappel & Benjamin Kanderson for the north-end of their Howland Closes being undone – each 1s 6d

[7.]   James Thompson for obstructing an Old Water Course in the West Common Lane – 5s 0d

[8.]   Joseph Perfect for the North side of his Garden being insufficient – 1s 6d

[9.]   Mr. Bridges for his dyke in the Town Street being undone – 0s 6d

[10.] John Winter for his bridge in the Town Street being insufficient – 0s 6d

[11.] John Middlebrough for the North side of his Close against Mark Daniel's Closes being undone – 5s 0d